ULTIMATE
CONVERSATIONS

THE BADDEST FIGHTERS
ON THE PLANET

BY FIAZ RAFIQ

ULTIMATE
CONVERSATIONS
THE BADDEST FIGHTERS ON THE PLANET
BY FIAZ RAFIQ

DEDICATION

This book is dedicated to none other than the ultimate fighter himself, the one and only, Royce Gracie, who changed the world of combat sports forever. A true inspiration, gentleman, unique human being, and a legend in the combat sports world with a heart of a lion. Without Royce Gracie there would never be UFC and the sport of MMA which we enjoy today.

Hardback ISBN: 10 DIGIT: 09552648-8-X
Hardback ISBN: 13 DIGIT: 978-0-9552648-8-7

Designer: Martin Jennings
Published by: HNL Publishing
A division of HNL Media Group
Suite 185, 6 Wilmslow Road, Manchester, M14 5TP. United Kingdom
Email: contact@hnlmediagroup.com

Distributed by:

UK	USA/CANADA	AUSTRALIA
PGUK - 8 The Arena,	Midpoint Trade Books.	Tower Books.
Mollison Avenue, Enfield.	27 West 20th Street. Suite 1102.	PO Box 213, Brookvale
Middlesex. EN3 7NJ.	NEW YORK-NY 10011	NSW, 2100

Front cover: photos courtesy of Punishment Athletics, Bladerunner and Michael Bisping
Back cover: photo courtesy of Cage Rage

ACKNOWLEDGEMENTS

I would like to thank many of the friends and people who have played an integral role in the success I enjoy today.

A big thank you to my magazine editor at 'Martial Arts Illustrated' Bob Sykes, who is not only the best editor but above all I am proud to call him one of my best friends. Without Bob I would have never achieved many of the things I set out to pursue. Thank you for being on my side and above all for your friendship. I look forward to our camping trip.

Thanks to Royce Gracie for years of friendship, support and the 'chokes'- 'you're the man' amigo! Thanks to Michael Bisping for his support and friendship. Diana Lee Inosanto and Ron Blaicki for their long lasting friendship and support over the years. Thanks to Dorian Yates, Tony Sykes, Ronnie Green, Kevin Morris, Sandy Holt, Karl Tanswell, Peter Consterdine, Master 'A', Gareth Williams and Mal Leadon, Seyfi and Abdul, Steve Marsden and his lovely wife, John Dawson and his 'crew' , Bernard, Salvatori and Nikol at the CVBBA, for their friendship and support.

Special thanks to Barry at Blade Runner, Steven Beale, Jimmy Page, Simon Yeo, Matt Freeman at MMA Unlimited magazine. All the staff at M.A.I and Impact magazines from Moira, Martin, Vicky, Beth, Neil and John Mosby who have treated me like a family. Tito Ortiz, Cindy and Megan at Punishment Athletics, Kevin at BRW, Mike Kogan, Mike Leeder, Rorion Gracie, Geoff Thompson for his advice and inspiration and Felix at 'Dorian Yates Ultimate Formulas'. I would like to thank all the professional fighters, martial artists, Boxers, Bodybuilders and personalities in the movie industry I've interviewed over the years and some of their agents and managers. A big thank you to PGUK and MTB for many years of support.

Thanks to Cage Rage's Dave O'Donnell and Tony, Alan Orr, Claire Atherton, Frank Shamrock Inc, Michael Bisping, Blade Runner, Rodrigo Gracie, Punishment Athletics for providing some of the photographs.

CONTENTS

FOREWORD
BY ROYCE GRACIE

My brother brought the Ultimate Fighting Championship concept from Brazil to the United States. My father had been fighting in No Holds Barred competitions for a long time in Brazil. People in America and all over the world have always been curious to see who the best fighter in the world is.

There was no such thing as a MMA fighter, this did not exist. It all started when the UFC was introduced. From the beginning it was one man representing his martial arts style against another. Today, everybody is an all round fighter, you see strikers practising grappling and the grapplers implementing striking into their game. The sport of MMA has come a long way to get to where it is today. It's not something that suddenly cropped up yesterday. The sport is no doubt going to grow even more.

This book is a great concept and Fiaz has compiled a good book for anybody interested in knowing 'who is who' in the sport - which includes both, the early fighters and the new generation of fighters.

FOREWORD
BY MICHAEL BISPING

Over the last few years the sport of mixed martial arts - in particular the UFC - has exploded from a cult following sport to a mainstream phenomenon with all major forms of media covering the sport from newspapers, magazines, ESPN, Spike TV, and the internet. This is the fastest growing sport in the world. The sport has helped transform martial artists and fighters from regular hard working fighters in the martial arts to bona-fide celebrities and household names.

In the early years of the sport people didn't give the sport and the fighters the respect they deserved, often disregarding them as thugs. Common misconception where people thought UFC fighters were straight from a bar stool into a fight. Thankfully these days with the right exposure the sport has received the world realises these fighters are highly trained athletes and experts in several different styles of martial arts disciplines and world class athletes in their own rights.

From my own personal experiences from being a normal working guy having worked average working class jobs 'The Ultimate Fighter' series and the UFC has completely transformed mine and my family's life.

In 'Ultimate Conversations' you will get to experience a one on one conversation with 25 of the baddest fighters on the planet. Find out what makes the fighters tick, find out some of the secrets from their careers and hear the fighters discuss the highs and the lows of their careers and find out what it takes to be an ultimate fighter. This book is compiled in a unique way and is definitely a first. In my opinion, for any combat sport or mixed martial arts fan this book is a must have. It gives you a true insight into the minds of your favourite fighters.

FOREWORD
BY BOB SYKES

I find myself more and more drawn towards mixed martial arts, now more than ever. It's no secret that in this style of combat any other discipline can match itself against another. It has, in fact gone well beyond that point, no longer do boxers fight wrestlers etc, instead a blend was formed which produced athletes who could fight in all ranges.

In this book, Fiaz Rafiq successfully captures this blend, a blend responsible for producing what could well be described as the world's most sought after fight game, to the point where it's even become bigger than boxing.

- Bob Sykes - editor of the UKs bestselling martial arts magazine, 'Martial Arts Illustrated'

INTRODUCTION
By Fiaz Rafiq

In less than a decade, the Ultimate Fighting Championship (UFC) and the sport of mixed martial arts (MMA) has gone from a novelty spectacle to a worldwide phenomenon. MMA is the world's fastest growing sport, seen in over 170 countries with over 300 million fans. The UFC went onto brake the pay-per-view industry's all time records. The sport has become so popular that it has even knocked boxing from the top spot in America, as the most popular combat sport. Furthermore, in the UK it is outselling cards headlined by such elite names as Ricky Hatton and Amir Khan. In Japan and the US, MMA has climbed to celestial heights with record attendances. It's not uncommon to see 100,000 fans packed in the Tokyo Dome for a big MMA fight.

When the first UFC debuted in November 1993, many people were outraged to see two combatants pitted against each other fight in a cage with no rules, protection or time limits. This eventually lead to accusations of brutality and for the sport to be labeled by many as 'human cockfighting'. This was when modern No Holds Barred emerged in popular culture, which had been made famous by the Gracie family in Brazil. Rorion Gracie, the eldest of the Gracie brothers, had been chasing the American dream when he moved to California as a teenager. After many years of struggle and overcoming obstacles, Gracie finally managed to stage a No Holds Barred competition in America (UFC I) which was an instant success. His younger brother Royce would showcase the extremely effective Brazilian Jiu-Jitsu skills in the octagon which changed the way the world perceived fighting forever. This was the beginning of the MMA phenomenon which would take the world by storm and propel it to an elevated level for years to come.

Soon the UFC organisation had to reform itself and adapted to stricter rules; indeed, athletic commission sanctioned rules. This was almost essential for the sport to survive and evolve, although the original concept envisioned by Rorion Gracie was left far off the mark. As a result of overall evolution of the sport, professional training camps, improved cutting edge training methods and a better understanding of the multiple disciplines, the fighters have become well rounded and respected athletes. The intense training these fighters endure and the need for technical excellence required to compete in such a tough sport makes these gladiators the hardest training athletes in the world. They push their bodies to the limits and train for up to six or eight hours a day.

Human Cockfighting
Or Spectacle Sport

Greg Jackson of the 'Jackson's MMA' camp is one of the more prominent coaches today who trains some of the elite UFC fighters explains why fighters are often intellectuals, as well as being the toughest athletes in the world.

"Absolutely, we are the hardest working athletes. First and foremost, the important thing is there is an art in every single part of our game. You have to know the art of boxing, the art of kickboxing, wrestling, jiu-jitsu, ground and pound - which is an art in itself - there are so many different disciplines you have to be aware of and you have to be an intellectual person to compete in this sport. It might not always look that way, but you have to understand all the pieces of the puzzles and the more beautiful it becomes. So it's very important to understand that there are intellectual parts. Also, physically, you have to get in there and wrestle, kick box, do jiu-jitsu for 15-25 minutes, that's an extremely tough environment to put your body into. You have to be mentally tough and physically in shape."

I asked him what his thoughts were of a street fighter who had no formal MMA training who got into the octagon. Could an untrained fighter from the street survive against the athletes who have pushed their bodies to the limits, honed their skills and competed at the highest levels in what has been called the toughest sport in the world? Jackson's answer was refreshing to say the least.

"You can't play tennis three or four times as a kid and expect to play at Wimbledon, it doesn't work that way. So, street fighters don't really mean anything because they're fighting people who have not got a lot of experience. Like any sport, you can play soccer as a kid but it doesn't mean you're going to win the world cup. It's a long process you have to pay a lot of dues. As an untrained fighter even if you get towards the top you'll be exposed to a lack of skills eventually. So you can't just hop into it, like every other sport you have to have skills. I would say there's no doubt MMA fighters are the hardest training athletes because of the physicality of it you have to have all the endurance and attributes. You know, soccer players run a lot, tennis players are explosive, but they're not getting some one punching them in the face for 15 minutes. You have to have that physical and mental toughness that other sports don't. Without a doubt MMA athletes are the toughest."

It is always interesting to see what the media's views are on something that has been labeled as controversial for many years. I asked FHM's Steven Beale what he thought of people who made such blunt comments as UFC fighters being compared to some untrained bar brawlers.

"I think if somebody said that, it would be an extremely ignorant comment. Anyone who says that doesn't actually mean it. We all have enough cultural experience of martial arts which involves a huge amount of discipline and artistry. A lot of people watch the Iraq wars on television and they say they could never ever do that. I think when people say that about bar fighters a lot of them are covering up their own insecurities.

I'm not saying this in a derogatory sense but it's a common feeling. It's also that people find difficult to align a trained skilled athlete to what they see as a brutal sport. It also depends what fight you watch, you can see some fighters like Bruce Lee in the movies and you can see other fighters who are quite clumsy fighters, as well as human cockfighting. I think the UFC is professional in the way they put their brand forward. If you watch other promotions - in particular one, I won't mention the name - you would quite easily be thinking its human cockfighting. I'm not talking about the fighters themselves but more about the way the sport is represented by certain people."

Beale continues enlightening me on the subject of MMA fighters showing respect and discipline and being good role models for kids in today's society.

"The rules have changed considerably; before, in the early days, they had no rules, no referee and you had your corner throw the towel in. In the early days, elbows to the top of the head were allowed. I think you have to put it in perspective, remember as much as we have these violent films or computer games, people aren't used to real violence at all. I think putting it in perspective, you'll see that it doesn't actually hurt that much. If the fighters are hit, they're used to it, it's not as brutal as you may think. Obviously, you still wince when you see someone doing a heavy ground and pound. I think what you have experience as an adult you kind of realise … and this is by the behaviour of the majority of the competitors which in itself people imagine a lot. They (competitors) are very honourable, their behaviour and respecting the opponent. It's a combination of chemical powers, courage combined with almost a code of honour and behaviour of the competitors, which is really refreshing. It's very good as a role model for kids as well. Basically kids have had role models who were bad guys, in particular Gangster rappers, for years kids have been told you have to be bad to get ahead and be on top. I think with the UFC it shows you can be a good guy and tough".

The Sport For The Future

The UFC is currently undergoing a remarkable surge in popularity and already grabbing a huge market share from boxing. The sport of MMA has penetrated the defence of the mainstream media after much adversity and criticism in the past. The rise of the number of spectators can no doubt be attributed to the power of the mainstream media. Dana White believes that 'The Ultimate Fighter' series played a major role in exposing the sport to a much wider audience and educating them. It's broadcast on Spike TV constantly ranking #1 in their time slots. The UFC has infiltrated into Europe and in particular the U.K. The raw, ruthless sport of MMA has become a breakthrough phenomenon beyond the scopes of the US. Not long ago the UFC purchased the top Japanese MMA show 'Pride Fighting Championships'.

The Japanese organisation had been showcasing to the world, just how popular and technically graceful the sport could be. MMA in the land of the rising sun set an early benchmark as far as popularity, acceptance and understanding goes by the fans. So just how big can this get? Will we see a rise in popularity and will it truly be considered as a mainstream sport. UFC fighters have no doubt broken into the mainstream media and the efforts of the media and the UFC itself, with its strategic marketing plans, has brought the sport to the attention of the ordinary man who may well never had an interest in the martial arts or never stepped into a gym. Steven Beale explains.

"I'm one of these people that think it'll go on and on and be as big as soccer. Well, not necessarily soccer because it's easier to get together with a few friends in the park, maybe I'll take that back. Certainly as big as boxing, probably more so. It's a lot more exciting than watching boxing, everyone knows that. I don't want to put boxing down because boxing is a very skilled art in itself. I think the international angle is very important. Whether you talk about the prominent stars or Eastern European fighters, the French, Scandinavian fighters,

Canadians, South Americans and Americans. I'm sure we'll get people from all countries, even India, China and South Africa."

The UFC has already created super stars who are idolised by their legions of fans. Today the fighters are treated like royalty. We can see bigger sponsorship deals, professional management, endorsements that go beyond the scope of sports products. MMA survived for many years without any mainstream attention; now with its mainstream coverage the sport has mushroomed into big business, catapulting its fighters to stardom around the globe. Professional promotions and management is required to maintain and elevate the overall growth and acceptance of the sport, just like any other sporting fields. Ken Pavia was a sports agent for 12 years; he managed professional baseball and hockey players, before moving into MMA management. His firm, 'MMA Agents' is based in Huntington Beach, Southern California and currently manages 51 fighters, of which, 31 are current and previous UFC fighters. He says his niche isn't taking on up-and-coming fighters who have the potential to break into the sport, but to take on athletes who have achieved a significant level of success on an upper level and bringing them up to an elite level.

"I think now there's money in the sport; there's much greater exposure with television and pay-per-view. Mainstream sponsors like Budweiser, Harley Davidson have really helped the sport, but that being said, I think you had a lot of characters in the early days who were just paying a couple of bucks to the fighters. In that sense, today you see guys who are very technical, who are very protective about what they do, very cautious and the money is bigger. I think the sky's the limit. Pay-per-view right now in MMA is beating and exceeding boxing. The boxers are compensated to a much higher degree, that being said the whole pay structure in boxing is much different compared to MMA. I think eventually, as time goes by, with proper management, the money will grow and be distributed more accurately. I believe that now some guys at the lower end are training for months and they're living in poverty and some have a second job, whilst promoters make millions and millions themselves every show. In baseball the average salary in the past, in the 81th position was $150,000 and 89th was $600,000 and today its 3 to 4 million. Basically, the revenue was profitable but the money was distributed differently. I think, in time and through proper management, the fighters with smart agents will ensure the money will be distributed accordingly."

We have seen a meteoric rise from obscure No Holds Barred fighting to record setting pay-per-view giant embraced by the media and millions of thirst hungry fans around the globe. UFC on Spike TV in the US and Setanta sports in the UK, EliteXC on major network CBS, the world of mixed martial arts has never been bigger. The sport is not a fad that will disappear in the years to come, it is here to stay. As long as the fans are hungry for action and the UFC continues to bring out new generation of stars, the sport will continue to exceed limitations and be enjoyed by millions of fans.

The Baddest Fighters On The Planet

Before the UFC exploded onto the scene boxers were highly respected fighters and regarded in high esteem. The world heavyweight boxing champion was no doubt considered as the toughest guy on the planet. The world of martial arts and Olympic wrestling has always taken a back seat when it came to mainstream exposure and acceptance by the average sports fan. The UFC has created super stars out of fighters who have gained respect and have been accepted as exceptionally gifted athletes. This fascinating book gives you an incredible glimpse into what it takes to survive in the world's most brutal arena, and what motivates these men and the challenges and hurdles they have to overcome to make a name for themselves. Within the pages of this tome are 25 of the top UFC fighters and champions to have ever stepped into the octagon and some of the hottest new prospects from radically diverse backgrounds giving us, in their own words, a rare personal insight into their lives and careers.

These elite titans are responsible for propelling the sport of MMA to a wider audience, making it the most exciting combat sport and the fastest growing sport in the world. From the legendary iconic figures, like Royce Gracie and Ken Shamrock, to the super stars Chuck Liddell and the 'Huntington Beach Bad Boy' Tito Ortiz, you will discover many untold truths. Then we have stars such as Rashad Evans, Brock Lesnar and the UK poster boy, Michael 'The Count' Bisping who have made names for themselves and continue to rise up the ranks of a sport that has changed their lives.

For those of you who want to get an insight into just what a UFC fighter is all about, you won't be disappointed. I wanted to compile a book in a way which has never been done before. With the sport being made available to a bigger and more mainstream audience, more and more people have formed an interest in knowing more about their idols. I think it's a great concept to have the top fighters of the sport in a single tome tell their stories, which will inspire many. It can be argued there are a number other names that belong on the list. However the fighters that are in this book are no ordinary fighters; they are the elite and the biggest names in the game, past and present. These are some of the great UFC champions and the hardest men in the toughest sport that has taken the world by storm.

ROYCE **GRACIE**

Royce Gracie is the greatest ever UFC champion and the God-father of mixed martial arts. Gracie shocked the world by entering the fist UFC in November 1993 by beating much bigger and stronger opponents. He started a revolution around the world proving the effectiveness of his superior style of jiu-jitsu. Gracie was crowned UFC champion a total of three times, before exiting the UFC after his super fight with Ken Shamrock in UFC V.

Five years later, he began fighting in Japan , his most memorable fight being with the Japanese legend Kazushi Sakuraba. Gracie is the most unlikely looking fighter you'll ever lay your eyes on, but behind that smile and mild mannered approach lies a technical skill and fighting spirit matched by very few. Various Hollywood celebrities have taken private lessons with Gracie, and he has taught law enforcement agencies defensive tactics. He continues to fight professionally.

Q: Royce tell me about your father, a weak looking man weighing 135 pounds, who revolutionised No Holds Barred fighting in Brazil ...

Royce Gracie: He based his style on leverage and positioning. It's about reality, self-defence, where you learn about defence and how to win a fight. You have to commit to not losing and, once you don't lose, the question is; how are you going to win the fight? He beat everybody, he fought in open weight divisions, he was only 135 pounds and was beating guys double his weight, beating everybody up and sending them to the hospital. This year he's going to be 95 years old. He challenged the heavyweight boxing champion, Joe Lewis; we have a letter from Joe Lewis declining. He said that he would fight anybody but wouldn't fight an MMA fight. My father would punch and beat his opponents up pretty hard. I asked him, "How come you beat your opponents up so much?" and he said because he would tell them to get off him but they wouldn't get off him, so he had to beat them up. I said, "OK, I understand that!" [laughs]

Q: Tell me about when you arrived in the U.S to help spread the word with your brother!

Royce Gracie: I grew up in Brazil until I was 17 years old and I came to America to live with Rorion. I went to school in Brazil and trained in jiu-jitsu. When I arrived in America I didn't know how to speak English, the only words I knew were 'stop' and 'like that'. I would teach a class using those two words. I would say 'stop' and then I would show the move and say, 'like that'. I started teaching classes and that's how I pretty much started learning English. We had Chuck Norris who took classes with us and Jim Kelly, professional baseball and football players would come and take our classes. They realised that this was something real and understood what we were talking about. So a friend or a student of theirs would bring a professional athlete and try out and take the first class and fall in love with our art.

Q: Let's talk about the famous Gracie open door challenge, which took place in the academy and the garage!

Royce Gracie: The Gracie challenge is where we had an open challenge but some people misunderstand the concept, thinking it's just about, "If you can beat me, I'll pay you money." It's not that way, most of the times there was no money involved but if someone wanted to make a personal bet with money that's OK; whatever you put on the table we'll match it.

Back in the garage days, even after that at the academy, the students got so hooked on Gracie Jiu-Jitsu they'd go out and tell their friends who may have been a karate instructor and say, "I've got a guy from Brazil, they'll fight anybody!" So the instructor or fighter would want to see what they could do.

They'd come in to the academy or garage and we would tell them our style's the most complete self-defence system, you can kick or punch but if I get in a clinch and take you down, you don't know what to do. Oh man! The thing we started. The opponent would say, "You'll never take me to the ground, because all my life I've never been taken to the floor before." So we would say, "Let's do it." So the whole challenge thing started.

A student or a friend of a friend, or a karate instructor wanted to check it out and we had a challenge right there. I fought this kung fu exponent who had read about us, 'The Gracies', and we were willing to prove our style is the best, so he phoned the academy and said he wanted to try us out and came in. He'd been training in kung fu all his life and he wanted to prove his style against ours. We said, "Sure". So we made an appointment and he came in and I embarrassed him.

Q: Tell me about the first UFC which was the backbone of the success we see today.

Royce Gracie: The first UFC was exciting; it made history. That was a phase in history what people thought could not be done, putting 2 guys in a cage on live TV. Rorion pulled that off, man.

The whole idea of building the UFC was to prove that Gracie Jiu-Jitsu was the best martial arts and fighting style. So by training all my life I was ready to battle against different styles and show that Gracie Jiu-Jitsu was the best style out there. Knowing what I'm doing and what Gracie Jiu-Jitsu is all about, I had enough confidence in myself and technique. I knew I was prepared to fight against a boxer, kickboxer or a wrestler.

Gracie Jiu-Jitsu was a complete art. It was karate versus kung fu, Gracie Jiu-Jitsu against a kickboxer, sumo guy versus a savate fighter. When they went to the ground they didn't know what to do, and other arts like judo and wrestling didn't know what I know. That's the main difference.

In today's fighting, everybody knows Gracie Jiu-Jitsu so, everybody knows how to kick and punch and wrestle now. Before they didn't, today they are athletes and fight to see who's the best, everybody trains stand up and grappling. It's not one style versus another style; it's more related to the person who can deliver his game. After the UFC's, I didn't change much, I'm still the same man, still today I know where I came from and I'm the same person as I was back then. Of course, we got more students, even after my last fight a lot of Brazilian Jiu-Jitsu schools gained students, which is good.

Q: Do you feel you proved to the world that a smaller guy could beat a much heavier and stronger guy when you beat Ken Shamrock, who weighed 240 pounds and looked ripped?

Royce Gracie: Not just that, his art wasn't a complete art, he admitted he got caught and later said "I got caught by surprise I didn't expect this skinny guy from Brazil to know more grappling than me." He was out-grappled, his size was OK, he's big, but the elephant isn't the king of the jungle. The first fight I had with him Shamrock came to fight me and I beat him in less than a minute, 56 seconds. I choked him.

As soon as he tapped, I let go of the choke and then he

said he did not give up; he's a liar. So I looked at the referee and said let it continue, we are going to continue and I said to Shamrock, "Are you ready? Lets go, keep going!" I was ready to make a move and choke him out for good. But then he was like, "You're right, I quit, I quit."

In the second fight, the rematch, we fought again, he's 240 pounds, I was about 180 at the time. He took me down, I pull the guard, he got on top of me, all he did in the fight was hold me for 30 minutes. I was trying to go for chokes and arm locks, even his father who was in his corner kept saying, "Stop hugging him, beat him." His own father, because he wasn't doing a thing. He hit me once with a punch. He was just holding me down, that's a shame somebody who is 240 pounds and a lot heavier.

When the fight was over it was declared a draw because nobody quit and he's saying to everybody because he hit me once that he's the winner. Shame, the guy is more than 50 pounds heavier than me. If I'm fighting at 180 pounds fighting 50 pound lighter than me and I can't finish that person then that person won. If you fight someone 50, 60 pound lighter and it's a draw I'll give it to the lightweight guy, I don't know where he got the idea that he won the fight, but he's not living on this world man. When I fought Dan Severn he did not know how to finish me, he could pin me down but he was wrestler. A lot of judo and wrestling everybody cross trains now, learning how to take down, clinch, submit, you have to do the stand up, and the boxing.

Q: What do you think of the concept of judges decisions, and why was it necessary to implement rules and regulations in the UFC after you exited?
Royce Gracie: Sometimes the judges' decision, one judge goes one way and the other one, the other way; it's very common. I prefer the fighters to decide the fight instead of the judges deciding. It depends what background you come from, if you

are a stand up fighter you're going to punch more, the gloves are there to protect the fighters hands not the opponents face, so without the gloves you may break your hand and not be able to punch again for a while. A lot of people break their hands even with the gloves, but the boxing gloves protect the hands not the opponent's face. When I was fighting in the UFC there were no gloves, no rules, no time limits so the new owners got together with boxing commission and the only way to make the whole thing legal was they had to have gloves and some rules. It was either that or the boxing commission banning the UFC because it was too brutal.

Q: How do you stay so focused before a fight?
Royce Gracie: I don't get overwhelmed by the crowds or the size of the crowds, or crowds cheering me or booing me, I'm pretty much in a neutral phase. It doesn't matter whether I'm in another place or location, or the crowds are for or against me. I just connect to myself and I'm on my own stage. In Japan, they have a lot of fans over there, people think all Japanese do martial arts but there are a lot more fans and they appreciate the fights and the finer technique that is demonstrated in the MMA fights.

Q: You have battled opponents weighing as much as 490 pounds. When you face some one as big as that who looks mean and who can bench press 500 pounds, what keeps you so cool and calm?
Royce Gracie: I know what I train for and what I'm capable of doing, how far I can go. If I showed you pictures of the training camp, I did exactly what happened in the fight when I trained that way in my training camp. The way I train at the training camp, that is what happens in the fight. My toughest fight was with [Kazushi] Sakuraba in Japan, which lasted 1 hour 45 minutes. Again this fight made history. He's a very tough opponent. It's good to be strong but it's not what is going to win

the fight, man. If you don't have the technique and don't know what you're doing you have no business in the ring. So you have to know what you're doing, once you do then strength can help. You can have the fastest car in town but if you don't have gas you're not going anywhere.

Q: What motivates you to fight?
Royce Gracie: I know what I'm doing that's the main thing. What motivates me to fight? To shut up the crowd who are talking trash and prove that I'm still here.

Q: You challenged Mike Tyson and he was invited to fight in the UFC, can you tell me how this challenge came about?
Royce Gracie: People think boxers are great athletes that they're the toughest in the food chain, but they are not the best fighters, they are the best boxers. Mike Tyson at the time was the best boxer, but not the best fighter, there's a difference. When we invited him to fight in the UFC our aim was to see who's the best fighter and said to him to come into the no-rules game and let's see what happens. He declined. I have nothing against boxers, I train in boxing too, they are great athletes, top of the food chain; the shape you get doing the boxing work out is unreal. But they are not the best in fighting.

Q: How do you feel that the thing you started has now become a big phenomenon?
Royce Gracie: Its getting there, people always are interested in seeing who is the best fighter, people like that, it's in the human nature, it's going to grow, man. Before, grapplers were not considered martial artists, but this changed after the UFC.

Q: Tell me about some of the celebrities you have taught such as Nicolas Cage and Guy Ritchie!
Royce Gracie: Yes, they are big fans of the sport. They want to know how to protect themselves, not to become professional

fighters, but for knowledge. Not to use it in the movies or anything like that, but gain knowledge as a person and for self-defence if someone picks a fight. That's why everyone looks for Gracie Jiu-Jitsu. It's to learn how to defend yourself.

Q: Were you supposed to train Brock Lesnar? And, which fighters impress you?

Royce Gracie: Brock Lesnar was so far away man it didn't work out, he's in a different state, it wasn't convenient for him to fly over to LA, maybe he didn't need it. Some of the fighters I'm impressed by are Anderson Silva, Lyoto Machida, Antonio Nougueira, Wanderlei Silva; I like the Brazilians, they're sharp, man.

Q: You look like the typical average guy on the street, you don't look like a fighter but are one of the most dangerous fighters on the planet!

Royce Gracie: One time, my brother said to me, "In a perfect world, you wouldn't be a fighter", and I looked at him thinking after all I've done.

I went home and after a week I called him back and said, "You're right, in a perfect world I probably wouldn't be a fighter." I never had a fight in the street, I'm not a mean person, all my fights are won in a kind of a nice way, where I'm not pounding my opponent's face inside out, I don't have to. So, yes, in a perfect world, I wouldn't be a fighter but the world isn't perfect [laughs]. If I want to be a fighter, I might as well be the best. I fight because I know what I'm doing.

Q: Lastly Royce, tell me about your traveling and training schedules, how do you fit everything in?

Royce Gracie: I spend about six months each year on the road, traveling and conducting seminars. I just got back from Israel, and I was in the UK for one day and in Ireland. In October, I'm back in England, Scotland, Ireland, Romania and its growing all over the world not just the USA . Everybody in the world wants to learn MMA. I get to travel around the world and do what I like, it's a great job man.

I've been on vacation for six weeks and I'm just getting back to work. When I've got a fight coming up I stop traveling and just concentrate on training. I implement stand up and a lot of grappling, check my opponent's weaknesses and strengths, and set up a strategy. I'm living my future, life's good.

KEN SHAMROCK

Ken Shamrock (born Kenneth Wayne Kilpatrick) is a living-legend and one of the pioneers of the sport of mixed marts arts. Like his adopted brother, Frank, the 'World's most dangerous man' also grew up in juvenile homes, an environment where you had to survive on a daily basis and fight to earn respect.

Shamrock made his UFC debut in 1993 in the first Ultimate Fighting Championship and fought his last fight in the UFC in October 2006. He has taken part in legendary and controversial battles with Royce Gracie, Tito Ortiz and Dan Severn. Shamrock's duels with Ortiz drew some of the biggest pay-per-view figures at the time.

He was a one-time 'Pancrase' champion and UFC super fight champion and also wrestled professionally for the WWE. Ken Shamrock is a UFC Hall of Famer who will no doubt be remembered as one of the leading figures and pioneers of the world's fastest growing sport. He is the founder of 'Lion's Den' MMA gyms.

Q: Ken, can you shed some light on your childhood?

Ken Shamrock: I grew up in Georgia and then moved out to California. I got into trouble when I was about ten years old and I got shipped off to different group and juvenile homes. I ended up in a place called the 'Shamrock Boys Home' with Bob Shamrock after I had stayed at several different places. I was 13 and-a-half years old, this was a time when I started learning how to change my ways. I graduated from school and went onto college. After junior college I went into the Marine Corps.

From that point on I got interested in professional wrestling and got involved. Then I had an opportunity to go to Japan to fight so that's when I actually got my first taste of mixed martial arts in Japan. It was called the UWF. My first fight was against a guy who I beat, and from that point I never looked back and went from fighting in Japan to the United States in the UFC to where I'm at now. Once I got into MMA fighting I never looked back, this was what I was made to do.

Q: When you were growing up did you get into trouble a lot?

Ken Shamrock: Well I grew up in group homes so you were always fighting, all the time, and I would fight for my territory and my space. I mean, I had to fight for my own respect, so it's something I did at a really young age when I was 10 years old. I was fighting all the time. Fighting to me was just kind of who I was, and what I was all about and where I grew up. I had to fight in order to keep anything I had and any respect I had. Then when I got into mixed martial arts and started fighting professionally, that was fun.

Q: Let's talk about your pro wrestling career before you got into the UFC...

Ken Shamrock: I got into pro wrestling in North Carolina where Gene Anderton and Nelson had a group there. I did very well for a year-and-a-half, and it was from here I got the opportunity to go to Japan to fight in MMA over there.

Q: How did you hear about the UFC and what steps did you take to get involved?
Ken Shamrock: I was actually doing mixed martial arts in Japan which was different than the UFC. When I first heard about the UFC I saw it was in a cage and it was closed fists and fights took place with no gloves. I remember thinking "I want to do that!" It was just another step up from what I was doing in Japan, where it was open hand strikes and submissions on the ground. When I got involved, there was this guy named Royce Gracie that everybody was talking about. I, of course, just blew him off, thinking he's just a karate guy wearing a gi, thinking I was the only one that knew any submissions.

I really didn't do much study on it and went in there thinking, I'm the best fighter out there and that I'll beat everybody. So I flew from Japan, after having a fight with Funakai - who I'd beaten in a minute and 40 seconds - to the U.S. three days prior to the UFC event into Denver, Colorado and fought.

I had my first fight with Patrick Smith who I submitted with a heel hook, then I fought Royce whom I thought was a striker who didn't know much grappling - and he wasn't that big either! I had no idea what the gi was used for and they took my shoes away which I had done grappling with forever. They wouldn't allow me to wear shoes, but allowed him to wear a gi. So I went in and I thought I had him in a submission hold but he wrapped his gi around my arm. Then, when I went for a leg lock, he pulled himself on me and wrapped his gi around my neck and choked me. From that point on, I was like "OK, these guys know how to cheat", so I'm going to learn how to defend myself from this cheating.

Q: What did you think of Royce, on the surface he doesn't look like a fighter but a normal looking guy?

Ken Shamrock: He's very deceptive, just like a normal guy who doesn't look like a tough guy, doesn't look very athletical but put him in a Gi and a ring and he's phenomenal .He's a wise guy and very good at what he does, and he proved it over the years that he was the 'man' when it came to grappling. So no one can deny him the credibility that he got through the UFC.

Q: When did you open the 'Lion's Den' gym which became one of the first MMA gyms?
Ken Shamrock: When I first started fighting over in Japan there was nothing over here in the United States where I could actually train both stand up and ground fighting. There was no such thing as the UFC at the time and no gyms around that actually did that type of training. You either grappled or you were a striker. So you had to go to different gyms to do specific training. I decided to develop a gym that would do both - train striking and grappling.

While I was over in Japan I trained at the dojo's. I put together my training facility where I would get a house and I would go out and find fighters and I would have a try out and once they made it in the team I would have them at the house where we would do the training. So I had a house full of fighters and all we did was train. That's how we developed the 'Lion's Den Team'. One day when I was watching a show on TV called 'Animal Kingdom'. They were showing and talking about how the lion was the king of the jungle. A lion would attack a running animal dig its claws into his back and neck, and it would pull it down in to the body. While the lion was on his back he would pull the prey down to his chest and bite its neck and kill it.

I thought, "What a great name, 'King of the Jungle', where you actually attacked the prey similar to grappling!" So I thought, 'Lion's Den' would be a good name. So I named the gym 'The Lion's Den', and started training fighters. We housed fighters and our guys would go out fighting and the 'Lion's

Den' had a reputation for having the toughest fighters out there and the only team in MMA that was fighting all the time. As you see now with 'The Ultimate Fighter' show, which is turned into a reality show which is what 'Lion's Den' did way before the TUF reality show came out. They took that and turned it into a reality show.

Q: On to your superfight with Royce Gracie in UFC 5 which was declared a draw, do you think had there been no time limits, it would have been a different outcome?

Ken Shamrock: There's no question about it. Royce Gracie was hurt, and carried out of the ring. He was the beat up fighter, there's no question about it. I was fresh and could have gone on a lot longer, but he was hanging on for the time to run out. He had so much damage to him, broken ribs, his eye was busted, his conditioning was low, he was pretty much saved by the bell. I think anybody who watched that fight knows that man got lucky, because there was a time limit in that particular fight. So, the question of, would it have been different? He would have lost. He lost that fight anyway; if you watch the fight anybody would say he got beat.

Q: How important is conditioning?

Ken Shamrock: No matter how good you are you can't win a fight unless you go in there and fight. So you have to be able to do that, conditioning is number one.

Q: Were you ever influenced by Bruce Lee?

Ken Shamrock: I watched a movie called 'Enter the Dragon' and in the very first scene he's fighting some big dude and he gets the guy on the ground and jumps into an armbar. That's when I first saw an actual submission mixed in with the stand up fighting. Bruce Lee did it! Bruce Lee was actually one of the first guys who ever did the cross training where two combatants would fight on the ground and also standing up. Back in those karate days, people didn't go to the ground and fight, but Bruce Lee knew this was an important part of being a complete fighter.

Q: After you and Royce became the face of the UFC, did you want to go back to Japan and fight in Pride?
Ken Shamrock: I went to a bunch of different places to fight. I fought in Pride for a while and had good success there. I went from Pride to the UFC and at the time UFC was doing 40,000 [pay-per-view] buys and when I came back to fight Tito it did about 140,000 buys. With Kimo, we did 150, or 160,000 buys. And then with the second Tito fight it was huge numbers; ever since I came back in the UFC they sky-rocketed in the pay-per-views.

Q: You fought Tito Ortiz in UFC 40 in 2005, do you feel - no matter how good a fighter is - a lot of the times it's about who is the better fighter on the day?
Ken Shamrock: That's true too, but a lot of people don't understand at the time I had torn something, but because the fight was big and there was so much hype about it and so much anticipation on it I couldn't back out. So I had to do the fight and did it anyway. So after that fight was over, I went into surgery and had my knee replaced. There's a lot of things that happened when I fought Tito and even the second time I fought Tito; I blew my shoulder out and again I still had to do the fight because it was too close to the fight to back out and too much hype for the fight for me to step down. I had a lot of bad luck when it came to fighting Tito as I seemed to be always injured. You know what, that's not to take anything away from Tito, you do what you need to do and he won the fight and that's that.

Q: You and Tito seem to have had heated words at the press conferences before your fights, why did you both seem to have a problem with each other?

Ken Shamrock: I think Tito and myself know how the sport works. I mean it's not just two guys getting in there and fighting, that's a big part of it of course, but people that understand the sport want to know why we're fighting and want something for you to fight about. I give people a reason for wanting me to fight and my opponent something to fight about. I find something in every one of my opponent that I don't like and I will pull it out and make it public why I don't like this guy and people tend to want to buy the fight and want to watch it more. It's not fake, it's real. The aim is real, the reasons are real, I just tend to find those things and I bring them out, I don't ignore them.

Q: You and Tito were on the TUF series coaching, would you like to share any interesting stories?
Ken Shamrock: The pool thing where he thought he was such a good player is one of them. The whole time when they mentioned that we were going to play pool and the coaches would be competing against each other and there would be $10,000 for the coach that won. I, basically, kind of looked disappointed because I couldn't really play pool and Tito jumped out of the seat like he played pool all the time, like he's a hustler. Then I went in and basically cleared the table and he couldn't recover after that. He was just completely taken out of his element because he was jumping up and down with his team players like he was going to win it, but I smoked him.

Q: After the UFC you went back into WWE. Why go back to entertainment fighting after fighting for real?
Ken Shamrock: The thing is, the UFC at that time was having a lot of problems, they were in court all the time and getting banned from all these different places therefore the money was going down. So I couldn't even support my family through fighting, so I started looking for other avenues. Someone in Canada had approached me several times about me coming in

and doing stuff with the WWE and so once the UFC started having problems, I decided I had to make money elsewhere because I couldn't support my family at the time.

So the guy talked to me and we got together with Vince McMahon and started working out some deals. So I got involved with them and had a very good experience with the WWE, it was a great time when I was there and making money to support my family.

Q: What do you think of some of these WWE wrestlers making the transition into the UFC, someone like Brock Lesnar for instance?

Ken Shamrock: I think it's very difficult for these guys to make a transition, the sports evolved so much that the UFC fighters are all cross-training and have been for several years. They all have had a lot of amateur fights; it's not like in the early UFC days when guys were just starting to learn grappling, striking and getting their conditioning up. They were just starting out.

A lot of guys can just jump in and do it, fortunately for me I was already doing it over in Japan so I had knowledge of submission and knowledge of striking so I was able to go from the pro wrestling world into the UFC, and vice versa. I had already experience in both, which made my transition very much easier. But, for guys who are doing it now, it's not going to be that easy, it's going to be very difficult making the transition.

Q: You had bad experiences with your management at one point, how important is it to have a good manager in the sport of MMA?

Ken Shamrock: Oh, really is important, because you travel a lot and you're training all the time and you're always on the road. You don't know what you're being charged or where the money is all going, the sooner you find out things weren't going where they are supposed to go. You owe taxes here and there, it's very important that you have somebody managing your financial arrangements that you really trust because it's really easy for money to disappear and you not know about it for a long period of time. Then there's nothing you can do about it because the way it is being done is legal. So you just really have to make sure someone you can trust and make sure you are watching where things are going.

Q: How do you feel now that the UFC has been embraced more openly by the media and the general public; whereas in the early days it was promoted as No Holds Barred?

Ken Shamrock: I think it had a lot to do with the athletic commission who got involved and the rules came in. Everybody has rules which are followed and the fighters have their physicals before the fights. Sanctioning the sport and providing rules was a big thing for them to get in there and do this, and without them it probably wouldn't be at the stage it is today. It was good finding a way for the sport to survive - and for the fans to be able to watch without the fighters going in there and getting seriously hurt.

Q: You fought Dan Severn in two superfights, am I right in saying both of you never got on? What was the reason behind this?

Ken Shamrock: Well It was a lot... I mean, again trying to build fights, trying to have animosity towards my opponent because I didn't like him. So I kind of picked upon things that Dan Severn said. We had a rules meeting, he seemed cocky, which he was - and all fighters are to a point before a fight.

So he was talking about certain things and he kind of over-stepped his boundaries, where he was the challenger and I was the champion. He was getting a little ignored as I was getting more media attention and questions. He kind of got upset that he wasn't getting asked any questions and, therefore, we got into a confrontation in the last meeting and I told him,

"Don't worry about it because I'm going to kill you anyway", and he got up and walked out of the meeting. I went into the ring where I proceeded to kick the crap out of him.

Q: You did a lot of media by appearing on some top mainstream talk shows in America was this the transition of bringing the MMA to the attention of the mainstream public?

Ken Shamrock: I think I was the first one to actually do the cross over to mainstream media. I don't know, but I guess my character really kind of appealed to a lot of people and was able to cross over and get the MMA to audiences that, may be, wouldn't been able to be reached otherwise. Then when I crossed over to pro wrestling fighting in the WWE I was on mainstream TV and people were wondering where I came from. So they knew about this MMA fighter and they started to ask the question "What's MMA?" Then they started doing research on my background and people started watching MMA and started telling other fans. Then I went back from WWE into MMA and brought a lot of fans from that mainstream audience into the MMA world. For instance when the UFC was only hitting 40,000 pay per view buys and then I went back in the UFC we did 150,000 buys and this had a lot to do with the fact that I had brought a lot of the fans from the WWE world.

Q: Has the UFC knocked boxing off the top spot in the U.S. as the most popular spectator combat sport?

Ken Shamrock: Absolutely, I think we were new and it was definitely a sport that was talked about. Any boxer, wrestler or karate guy could get into the MMA and fight an MMA fighter and lose because he's not well-rounded. This thing about who is the toughest guy was proven in fact without talking but through actual fighting, and MMA always won because boxing is one dimensional, just as is wrestling and karate.

On the other hand MMA is multiple disciplines, all into

one. So, therefore, it was proven, "Hey, you know what this is the real deal? These are the real fighters!" People want to watch things that are real, that are the best, it was proven over and over with different disciplines coming into the UFC and finding out. You cannot be one dimensional, you had to know all disciplines. So boxing has now taken a back seat but boxing is a very good event, those guys are very skilled but UFC is hot right now.

But, like everything in life, what goes up must come down, nobody stays on top forever; everybody takes a turn. UFC and MMA will also go down again and boxing will pull back up again and probably be on top for a while and MMA will come back on top again and everybody will have its time and its place. It always does that, there's shifts and changes and it will always be that way in the world; nothing stays the same, and it can't stay the same, otherwise we would cease to exist. It's always the way the cycle of life works. So, therefore, we are on top right now, MMA is doing very well.

Q: Am I right in saying you had some trouble with the UFC in terms of your contract. Did they release you before it actually expired?

Ken Shamrock: It's something we have got to decide in the court of law, I don't want to get into it; for one, we're going to leave it to the attorneys. I've figured this thing out and I want to settle it in the court of law, so I can't really talk much about that. But everybody knows the kind of person I am, I don't get into situations like this - but when I am in a situation like this, it's usually because I'm provoked. So I just want to let the attorneys figure it out and hopefully we can get this figured out without it getting too nasty.

Q: Dana White turned the UFC around; there are fighters like Tito Ortiz and Randy Couture who believe there should be a lot more money for the fighters. How do you feel about this?

Ken Shamrock: There needs to be a fighter's union, so these guys have someone they can go to when they feel they have been wronged. Right now, I think the UFC wants to keep that out because they don't want us in their because this way they can keep all the money. Fighters are not getting paid the way they need to be paid, I think everybody knows that. But how do you get them paid?

The only way you can make it fair is to have a union, somewhere the fighters can go direct to but right now they don't have that. So therefore they don't have anybody fighting for them. The sport is young and it will take some time to have this in place. It will have to; otherwise it will cease to exist.

Q: You're currently 44 years old, what motivates people like yourself and Randy Couture to keep fighting? Would you consider taking other avenues such as coaching?

Ken Shamrock: There's no question about it, I want to get involved in other areas which I'm doing right now actually. I'll probably fight one more time, just so I can go out on my own terms and say goodbye to all my fans in the ring. But they'll be seeing me doing other things such as promoting fights, opening gyms, training fighters and I'll definitely be involved in this sport, but in a different way.

Q: Your son is fighting in MMA now, do you feel he'll go a long way? Does he have a future in this tough sport?

Ken Shamrock: Yes, he's a very tough kid, he fought in England which was his second fight and he broke his hand and still continued to finish the round and knocked the guy down with his broken hand and took him down twice. In my opinion he won the first round, but at the end of the round his trainer looked at his hand and he had a bone sticking out of his hand. It wasn't a fracture but a break, so he couldn't continue in the next round but the toughness and the skill he showed being such a young fighter was there. He's still inexperienced, but he still managed to win the round, breaking his hand 36 seconds into the fight.

He's still healing the hand, but once it does, he'll be back in the ring and I think people will enjoy his fights. I've got a nephew fighting this week in San Jose in the 'Strike Force' - he's 18 years old and is a phenomenal fighter too. So I've got two of my Shamrock boys going into MMA fighting and in probably three year's time, I'll have all of them in fighting.

Q: Will we see another 'Ken Vs Royce' fight again?
Ken Shamrock: We're hoping that will happen, I don't know if Royce will do it, but if he does I'll be happy to punch him in the head again.

TITO ORTIZ
'THE HUNTINGTON BEACH BAD BOY'

I n the late 90s, 'The Huntington Beach Bad Boy', Tito Ortiz emerged as one of UFC's biggest and most controversial stars. However, the former light-heavyweight champion had an extremely rough childhood where gangs and drugs were the norm. Even still, Ortiz excelled in wrestling as a teenager and made his UFC debut in 1997. He is famously known for his rivalries with the legendary Ken Shamrock who Ortiz beat three times; their fights drew record pay-per-view figures.

From April 2000 to September 2003, Tito successfully defended his light-heavyweight title until Randy Couture defeated him by decision at UFC 44. Ortiz was one of the major forces in making the sport exciting for the fans and his character appeals to millions. Ortiz's bad blood with UFC president Dana White made headlines after the fighter accused him of not paying the fighters what they are worth. Although he has exited the UFC he will continue to fight in MMA and has a number of business ventures which he manages.

Q: Tito, I understand your childhood was not the happiest time of your life. Tell me what obstacles you had to overcome in everyday life to survive.

Tito Ortiz: From the age of 7 to 13 my parents were drug addicts, but I was never using drugs with them, ever, but it was a factor of them using them and me going along with the 'ride'. It was really tough moving house to house, motel to motel and college to college. We had it really tough. My mom left my father and got remarried and I got a second chance of life I think. We lived in people's garages and couches, it got really rough for us. It wasn't until one of the gangs I was in, that one of my friends got shot and killed, that she came to realise that she better get me out of where we were living or I would be next.

When I was in high school I mixed with that gang culture really bad. So when one of my friends got shot and killed it was a chance for me to get out of all that from Santa Ana, a city here in Southern California which is very gang populated. I was always fighting every weekend and then guns started coming out of the fights. My mom got me out of that and brought me back to Huntington Beach. I kind of got my nose cleaned by getting into wrestling.

Q: Is it OK to tell me more about your involvement in wrestling?

Tito Ortiz: I got interested in wrestling in my freshman year in high school. I walked into the wrestling room because I was always a big WWE wrestling fan. I always wanted to wrestle, so I walked into the wrestling room and there was no ring, and I asked where the ring was. I came to realise that collegiate wrestling was totally different to professional wrestling. But I got attracted to it because it was a one-on-one sport. The harder I trained, the better I became.

Q: What were you doing to make ends meet?

Tito Ortiz: At that time I was actually working on a fishing boat, here in California. It was day times in the summer and night times in the winter. It was a full time job but just enough to make ends meet. When I got out of high school, I really had to make ends meet because I was on my own; my mom gave me 800 bucks and said, "It's time for you to be a man, time for you to grow up." I went out and bought a car and rented a house and just started finding jobs. Then this fight game came along from the wrestling.

Q: Can you recall when you first saw the UFC?
Tito Ortiz: I watched the very first UFC all the way up to the 6th one, I was nothing but a fan. And after the 6th UFC, when Tank Abbot fought, he trained where I was wrestling at. I was one of the better wrestlers in California, so he brought me in as a training partner. Then, from that point on, it was an evolution of the sport to what it is today and I was the front runner of all of it.

After I competed for a year-and-a-half in the UFC, I became a world champion, and after that one year after I defended my world title and became one of the biggest stars in the sport today. As a fan watching it back in those days, I thought these guys were crazy and I never really thought to myself I'd be fighting in the UFC in the future. These guys who were great athletes, like Royce Gracie who was choking the wrestlers out left and right. That was a turning point for me and I started learning jiu-jitsu and I've got to thank Royce Gracie for that.

Q: Was he a big inspiration to you?
Tito Ortiz: I think he was a huge inspiration to all of the athletes back then and even now. If it wasn't for Royce Gracie, no-one would know what jiu-jitsu was. Royce Gracie is an icon of mixed martial arts. He was the guy who brought the martial arts side to it, and then there's guys like me who brought the

spectacle side to it and made it interesting for the fans - to fall in love with their favourite fighters, like myself.

Q: You and Chuck Liddell were both managed by Dana White, tell me about the early relationship...
Tito Ortiz: The early relationship was always great; Dana White always had our best interests in everything we did. But as soon as he became the president of the UFC, it was the best interests of the UFC and not us, the fighters who got him there. I look at it as a disrespect, it just got worse and worse, where he cared more about the company and cared less about us.

In the beginning he was fighting for us, he said his fighters need 'this amount' from the pay-per-view and they need 'this amount of money' etc. And now I'm saying the same thing and Dana calls me a moron. I'm arguing for the same thing that he was arguing when he was my manager. Dana White is talking smack about me because I'm looking out for my best interests.

Q: You won the light-heavyweight belt in UFC 25 against Wanderlei Silva. What are your thoughts on achieving this milestone?
Tito Ortiz: For one, I slept with my belt for the first month after receiving it. It was great glory for me. After only being in the sport for a year-and-a-half, I beat one of the top light-heavyweights at the time, Wanderlei Silva, who only had a couple of losses on his record; he was just crushing through people.

Prior to this fight I fought Frank Shamrock and lost to him at the end of the 4th round, it was pretty much because of exhaustion. Frank Shamrock never wanted a rematch so they got the best light-heavyweight out there, probably one of the most dangerous guys, which was Wanderlei Silva. We fought for the vacant title belt and the best guy got his hand raised. Thank God, that was me.

Q: One of the toughest fights of your career was against Randy Couture, who beat you. You once related to me this was one of the saddest moments of your career, why was that?

Tito Ortiz: Losing to Couture when you are on top of the hill and you're the champion and everybody wants a piece of you. No-one says "No", to you and all of a sudden you lose it and you look in your dressing room, where, in the beginning of the fight there's 20 people in there, and after your loss there's only three in your room. You kind of realise how people react to losers I guess, it really hurt me because I didn't suffer a loss for almost four years and all of a sudden I lost and it felt like the world got ripped underneath me.

I compare it to a loved one dying when I suffered that loss. Couture fought a great fight. I got injured about a month before the fight with my lower back disc, so I wasn't even able to wrestle, but boxed and did jiu-jitsu, and that's what it came down to in the fight - he dominated me by outwrestling me, he finally got a takedown and dominated me. He didn't hurt me seriously, but he fought a fight, it was one of my worst losses I ever had.

Q: At one point people thought UFC fighters resembled street thugs. Do you feel UFC fighters are the hardest training athletes in the world?

Tito Ortiz: The competitors competing now are one hundred percent athletes. They are well rounded athletes not just in fighting, but marketing and interviewing. All these guys are educated and come from a college background. Like myself, Randy Couture went to Oklahoma State, Chuck Liddell went to Cal Poly here in California; [Quinton] Rampage [Jackson] went to college. All of us have got some sort of a college degree and a college career in wrestling. We thought we were going to be professional wrestlers. Now we are professional fighters and make the sport what it is today.

So the athletes that compete now are nothing like any other combative sport, just because the great athletes we are, we train six days a week, eight hours a day and we treat it as a full time job. We carry the whole business on our shoulders; everybody is watching what we do. We're getting mainstream each and every day more and more and as people watch us and understand what we do, they see that we are human, we do make mistakes and there's a lot of guys who take this job very seriously and it is a full time job. We're not bar brawling morons trying to pick a fight; we are athletes that compete in a sport which is growing each and every day.

Q: Let's talk about your rivalry with Ken Shamrock and his brother Frank!
Tito Ortiz: With Shamrock it all started off when I fought one of the Lion's Den fighters at UFC 13. I fought Guy Mezger and I was kicking his ass and he got me in a choke and he won the fight. I felt like I had to get revenge, so next time I fought Jerry Bolander I put on a t-shirt - it was a sponsor shirt - a porno company and it read on the back 'I just fucked your ass'; it wasn't meant personal towards Bolander at all, it was strictly a sponsor shirt and I made some money on it and I put the shirt on after the fight. Everybody assumed that I was talking about Jerry Bolander, which I wasn't, and this was the beginning of my rivalry with the 'Lions Den'.

Then I had a re-match with Guy Mezger and I put on a shirt after the fight which read 'Guy Mezger's my bitch' they didn't like it. I didn't have a 'Lion's Den' backing me up, I was myself with a couple of my trainers, but they had a whole team who trained with him. I wasn't going to back down to him, it was automatic, Ken Shamrock and his team started talking smack about me.

A couple of years later me and him had a chance to fight each other; the rivalry had already built up and we fought. I stopped him in three rounds and it got worse… He kept talking more and more smack and so we fought again. We did the TUF and built hostility on that and we fought again - and I stopped him in a minute and 18 seconds.

He said it was a premature stop, but I thought he was clearly knocked out. The UFC came to me and asked if I wanted to fight Ken Shamrock again and I told them I already beat him twice, but I said, "If the fans deserve to see it, then let's do it!" I stopped him for the 3rd and final time. We shook hands and let bygones be bygones; he's an acquaintance no more than that, its history now. We've gone on our own business ventures and we're separate people now.

Q: In one of the press conferences, Ken Shamrock lost his temper with you but you seem to stay cool and calm. How did you manage to do that?

Tito Ortiz: I think this happened in three or four of the press conferences actually [laughs]. I push the buttons, I do things that not many fighters can do to others. It's kind of like Ali and Frasier. Ali can talk as much smack as he can as long as he backs it up; I try to get into the guys head, and that's what I do. Like I said, there were a couple of press conferences which had these incidents. First fight, then when, after he fought Kimo, he talked some smack that he wasn't healthy and wanted to fight me again, and another opportunity came by at TUF where he tried to be a bully and try to push me around which wasn't happening, but we solved our differences in the cage - that's for sure.

Q: How did you find the experience on TUF?

Tito Ortiz: The experience was great and I got to train with some really great guys. Michael Bisping came out on top, number 1. He was leaps far above all the guys competing on the show. Me and Bisping have a good relationship now, he's actually out here in California training, I worked out with him yesterday and most likely work out today. Kendal Grove,

Matt Hamill were also on the show. A lot of normal fans got to see what kind of a coach I was.

Coaching is one of my secrets, I'm a good coach, I did coaching in the collegiate wrestling for high school students and college students. I understand the team game and the personal game to be better fighters and I think I showed a lot when I did TUF, and it helped me a lot. People used to say, "Tito Ortiz talks shit in the octagon", then they see that he gives back something and helps other fighters. In TUF, they got to see this side of me.

Q: You fought Chuck Liddell at UFC 47, is it true he said you tried to avoid fighting him?
Tito Ortiz: There was a lot of bullshit behind it because of the picture Dana White was painting. Chuck Liddell and I said we weren't going to fight each other unless we got paid big dollars. I tried to hold on as long as possible but Chuck Liddell sold out to the company not really caring about it; all he wanted was the belt.

For me, for a friend to fight a friend I thought we should be paid a lot of money. For him money is more important than friendship; that's fine, it shows what type of a person he is. The fight happened and I lost, shit happens, I made a few mistakes. I really think that blood is thicker than water, but he sold out. When you have a person staying at your house and I was staying at his house, you think there's a friendship built there, but Dana White painted a picture like there was no friendship. It kind of sucks, because we were good friends at that point.

Q: You are friends with another notorious fighter, Mike Tyson. Tell me about your friendship with the former heavyweight champ...
Tito Ortiz: Actually I met him when he fought Francois Botha, after that I gave him my punishment gear and he walked out

with a beanie hat, when he fought in England. He always came to my fights; I love the intensity of Tyson and the fighting style he has. Since I was really young, I've always been a huge supporter of Tyson and he's been a huge supporter of me so we have a great relationship.

Q: What are your personal views on a heavyweight boxing champion being labeled as the toughest guy in the world?
Tito Ortiz: It's like comparing apples to oranges. With boxing, it's like checkers and MMA is like chess. We have to move so many directions to win a game, boxers go forward and backwards... that's it. But MMA is a multiple disciplines, kickboxing, wrestling, Jiu-Jitsu, boxing, cardio and weight training. There are so many things you need to be a great athlete at. You can't just be good with your hands. There's so much stuff that relate to MMA.

Boxing is simple using two hands; a boxer wouldn't last a minute, any heavyweight, lightweight, middleweight champions, they wouldn't last a minute with any of the champions in MMA. Now let me give you kind of an idea, so people say boxing is always better. If I went and participated in a boxing match, I may last a round or two because I have a little bit of boxing experience. It's two totally two separate games.

Q: MMA evolved into a mainstream sport what are your feelings on this?
Tito Ortiz: When I started fighting back in the no-rules and no-time limits era, there were only 3 weight classes, lightweight, middleweight and heavyweight, that's it. But as you see, the sport evolved and became what it is today. It's just amazing knowing that I was one of the ambassadors of the sport making it what it is today. The athletes competing today are so well rounded, there are not just jiu-jitsu guys or kickboxers, a lot are really well trained in all areas.

In the beginning, they were so one dimensional but now

there's a lot to learn; that's why there's so many good fighters compared to the beginning. When I started fighting, in the beginning, there was 1500 people in the audience with may be 10,000 pay per view buyers; now there's 16,000 people in the arena and over a million pay per view buyers - so the sport has grown a great deal.

If two guys get into the ring and fight, this is something the fans want to watch and pay the money. Like I said, we're pretty much the modern day gladiators like back in the Roman days, that's why people are attracted to our sport.

Q: What are your views on Dana White and the UFC not paying enough money to fighters? Boxers get paid millions of dollars...

Tito Ortiz: Exactly, what it really comes down to is that the fighters who are making them the money need to be taken care of, and they're not taken care of. They take advantage of them, and solicit them and not pay them what they're worth. In boxing, the fighters are making 10, 20 million dollars per fight and we scratch up to get up to a million. They're making 30 or even 40 million an event; we'll bite them in the butt in the long run and I'm a person to stand up and make a difference. Muhammad Ali did for the boxing, I'm going to do the same thing in MMA.

Q: You started speaking up about the fighters deserving more money. Is it true that Dana White and his guys told you to be quiet and don't make a noise and they'll give you a little more money?

Tito Ortiz: That's very true, I thought it was going to get better and I wasn't going to say anything and all of a sudden Dana White started painting a picture that I'm a moron and I'm afraid of Chuck Liddell, and that I'm no longer a fighter and I want to be a movie star. He was just talking so much smack about me, it was just non-stop hindering my image. It degrades me 100%.

I couldn't handle it anymore, so I keep speaking out for what I'm really worth. These guys try to disrespect me, time and again, but I have great fans who are going to follow me no matter where I go. I'm really excited about what will happen in the future.

Q: You say that Dana White seems to want to be a star?

Tito Ortiz: He was the guy on Spike in a show showing Dana White flying in the jets, taking cars and doing the weigh - ins, he's doing the pictures and autographs and after the events he's doing the after-parties. You tell me that's someone who doesn't want to be a super star? He wants to be a star. He's doing all those things, soon he'll be fighting in the UFC that's the next step!

Now that I see [UFC co-owners] the Fertita's came in and started to clean up some of the stuff Dana has done, it just shows his desire at wanting to be a super star. Time again he wants to be at the forefront; the last fight between Forrest versus Rampage happened, it was all about the main two event fighters and 'Dana White'. Dana White hasn't even fought in the octagon but he's trying to be that champion and superstar. When you have a billion dollars behind you like he does, you can make that happen and Dana White's doing it.

Q: It seems he didn't want you to come to the press conference at your last fight and made every effort to keep you out?

Tito Ortiz: He didn't want me speaking out; he didn't want me to say what was true; especially, with all the fighters around him at the press conference. The authorities tried to hold me out of getting into the press conference, but this is the United States of America and we have the freedom of speech. I was stepping up and said what I believed in. I told them, "I'm staying here; you guys better get security to rip me out of here because that's the only way I'm leaving!"

Q: Why didn't the boxing charity bout between you and Dana go ahead?

Tito Ortiz: In the beginning, it was supposed to be for charity, he was going to keep the money all to himself he wasn't going to cut me into it. We had an agreement that we would go 50/50 on any revenue that grossed from this boxing event we had. Then, all of a sudden, when it didn't go down, I told him he tried to take advantage of me and use me to get himself to be a superstar. He said it was, "all for charity, so Tito isn't going to get any money." Once again, he tried to make me look bad and I didn't know anything about that. I thought it was going to charity and I said, "That's terrific, let's do it, then give all the money to the charity." But they dropped the ball on it because it wasn't going to happen.

Q: Would you honestly really like to beat your former boss up?

Tito Ortiz: Yeah, I'd like to beat him up as a street thug. Me and him just don't get along and if we did have a boxing match, he wouldn't last a round, he'd be lucky to last a round. The only way he would have lasted a round is if he ran around the cage the whole time. But if I got hold of him, I guarantee you I would have knocked his ass off. That's history now, I'm willing to move on in my career and think about all the good things I have in the future.

Q: Tell me about your appearance on TV show, 'The Apprentice'.

Tito Ortiz: My Punishment Athletics company started with 500 dollars and has grown to a multi million dollar company in the last 8 years, we've done really well. Donald Trump knew I was a great fighter and they wanted to bring a sports guy in - and they knew I was a good business man because of my clothing company.

I had a conversation and they told me it was for charity

and all the money I would raise would go to my favourite charity, which is St Hughes Children's Hospital. I got to raise $70,000, and build the awareness of the charity too. It was a good opportunity for me too, and the average fan who watches the UFC got to see Tito Ortiz the businessman, not just a fighter.

I also filmed a reality show, 'Anytown Beat Down', where we have a couple of guys who have a beef with each other, some stuff has happened between them when they were kids, or one guy had sex with his wife or something and they have hostility for each other. We teach them how to train for five days and they fight on the 6th day, solve the differences in the cage. It's similar kind of thing to TUF but these are people off the street, who have anger towards each other.

Q: Your last fight for the UFC was against Lyoto Machida, you nearly pulled it off when you had the triangle choke. What happened?

Tito Ortiz: I came to fight man, I was in great shape, and I came at him and he took me down in the first round but I got over anxious try to grab hold of him. In the second round he ran a lot more, then end of the third I tried to get hold of him but all he would do was try to run when I engaged to fight. He would take a punch and move back and forth, he was running the whole time.

Last time I saw a mixed martial arts match, we fight, we bring it on in the fight, we don't make it disinteresting for the fans; I've always been like that, making a fight interesting for the fans. But he would run... I got over-extended, he dropped me, got a couple of punches and I pushed his arm through and triangle lock. Then he got out of it because I switched to an arm lock.

Believe me, I kick myself every single day. No ones going to get out of my triangles ever again, I've been drilling them so much ever since that fight; its just one of those things where I can catch somebody in that position, they are not getting away. Machida got lucky, which is fine, he's undefeated - but who wants to watch a boring fighter who runs away the whole time and doesn't fight? It just shows where his career is going to be going.

Q: You stated once that you would fight Chuck Liddell five or six times if you had to - is that true?

Tito Ortiz: That was some time ago. My business ventures have changed a whole bunch. I may even not be fighting in the UFC ever again. I might be going to Affliction or EliteXC. Next month, I'll know 100% where I will be going. As far as calling UFC home... as long as Dana White is president, I'll never call that home.

I feel bad for the company and for all the fans who have watched me fight in the UFC, where I go they're going to follow and Dana White screwed that up. He wanted to be stingy with the millions instead of paying us the fighters more money. He says, "All you are stupid fighters." There was another interview he did in Rolling Stone magazine, where he was calling us morons, once we start to talk about money - we're all morons and we don't know what we are all talking about.

That is fine, I'm a business man and they want to negotiate certain ways, but I'll be looking elsewhere. About fighting Chuck Liddell, well he's going to be retiring pretty soon he's almost 40 years old, so he is near to end of his career, I'm only 33 years old, I'm still a young guy. Randy Couture started his career at 33, so my future is very bright and we're going to see where we go from there next.

Q: How do you see the sport of MMA growing, do you think it's overtaken boxing in the U.S?

Tito Ortiz: I think it has a life time left, in particular in the mainstream. In the next year, there are other companies coming about, finding other fighters. It's about the fighters, they are the ones that get into the cage and entertain the fans that watch. It's not the brand that's doing it, it's not the UFC, Affliction or EliteXC; it's the fighters showcasing their skills for the fans to watch.

So the next three years the sport is going to be huge. We're overtaken boxing and pro wrestling. We are the new brand sport now, we're true athletes, like I said, modern day gladiators, who people used to watch this type of fighting for thousands of years. We're in the right place at the right time and it's going to grow bigger.

Q: Who would you say is the god-father of MMA out of all of the fighters who have stepped into the octagon?
Tito Ortiz: You've got to think about it and I believe Royce Gracie as being the god-father of MMA more than anybody. He got in the cage and fought. Royce Gracie is the really true pioneer, and god-father, of MMA. I say the real god-father out of all of them has to be Royce Gracie without a doubt.

Q: Have you any final comments to add?
Tito Ortiz: I just want to thank all of my fans for the support buying the pay per view you know you're going to get an action packed fight no matter who or where I fight. My clothing company Punishment Athletics. We'll see what happens in the future, where and who I fight. I have some great business ventures which are going to happen.

RANDY COUTURE
'THE NATURAL'

Many consider Randy 'The Natural' Couture to be the most popular and successful UFC fighter in history. A member of UFC 'Hall of Fame', Couture was a very successful amateur wrestler, winning numerous championships and going on to become a 3-time Olympic alternate and a semi-finalist at the 2000 Olympic trials.

Couture made his UFC debut on May 30, 1997 at UFC 13 and, later in the year, 'The Natural' won the heavyweight belt by defeating Maurice Smith at the initial 'Ultimate Japan' event. Since that famous championship win, he has fought some of the biggest names in the heavyweight and light-heavyweight divisions such as Chuck Liddell, Tito Ortiz, Tim Sylvia and Vitor Belfort.

Couture has also pursued acting during his varied career, having appeared in a number of movies, include a role in a Steven Seagal movie, 'Redbelt' and a lead role in the upcoming, 'Scorpion King' movie. Couture is one of the most recognisable UFC fighters, and as such, has already played an important part in bringing the sport into the mainstream. He lives in Vegas and has a chain of MMA gyms around the country.

Q: Randy, when did you get involved in amateur wrestling?
Randy Couture: I started in grade school, my best friend's brother was wrestling; we went to one of the tournaments where they happened to have a novice division I think. I got my first broken nose competing in that tournament. My opponent put me in a headlock and I didn't know what a headlock was back then. I went through several stages, I obviously wrestled in school and won state championships in high school and I wrestled for the United States Army which I joined in 1982, and a couple of other championships and then the world championships.

I was also a 3-time Olympic team alternate from 1988 to 1996. I then wrestled at the Oklahoma State University for four years, I was an All-American 3-times runner up in Division 1. I started winning national titles in Greco-Roman wrestling, I ended up winning four national titles with the Pan-American teams and competed in world championships representing the United States.

Q: When did you first come across the UFC?
Randy Couture: One of the athletes I coached brought a UFC tape down and we put it in the VCR and started watching it. One of the guys I went to college with named Don Frye was fighting in the competition. I was immediately intrigued by the sport and sent in an application and the UFC rang up about six months later, with me finally getting the chance to compete in UFC 13.

Q: What did you think of Royce Gracie who was dominating bigger and stronger opponents?
Randy Couture: I didn't really tune into Brazilian Jiu-Jitsu and Royce Gracie till after my first UFC fight. I entered the UFC 13, after that I got a lot of background and studied it more. I entered as a wrestler first time and then realised I needed to learn a lot of stuff and started looking at Royce Gracie and

other jiu-jitsu practitioners and what they were doing and what their strengths were. Wrestlers started studying striking from boxing, Muay Thai and these boxing drills integrated into the wrestling background they had.

Q: How did it feel fighting in the UFC for the first time and was it a lot different to what you were accustomed to as a competitor?

Randy Couture: It was a lot different from what I was used to, the crowd was loud. Walking out there was pretty overwhelming. There were a lot of things on my mind, you go out and compete and try not to be over whelmed by the whole thing.

Q: Can you talk about your most memorable fights. Would you say this was against Chuck or Tito?

Randy Couture: I've probably had a few during my career, but probably the first memorable fight for me was my third UFC fight in October 1997 against Vitor Belfort who was pretty much untouchable at the time, this was a pretty memorable fight for me. The toughest fight I've been in is the Pedro Rizzo fight. I fought for 5 rounds and, to date, this is the toughest fight I've ever had.

Q: Can you shed some light on your training sessions before preparing for a fight?

Randy Couture: I like to peak 10 weeks before a fight. I study tapes of my opponent and decide what we think his strengths and weaknesses are and try to watch out for them. We get a game plan together; a lot of striking, sprint work, conditioning and I like doing a lot of sprint training, also lots of plyometrics. This topped with a couple of days a week real hard sparring where my partners try to wear me down - this is done with multiple partners. Other times, sparring and striking in different situations, worst case scenario training by putting myself in a potential worst position from where the opponent can put me in and I have to find a way to survive neutralise it, and try to win the fight. All-in-all, a well rounded approach.

Q: How much of a part does mental preparation play?
Randy Couture: I can't speak for the other fighters but certainly visualisation, controlling the voices in the head telling you that you are afraid, keeping your anger in control and you know what you need to do which are the mental skills that I try to practise. A lot of it is visualisation exercises and application exercises during the training cycle so you see what people are trying to do. I think it's a big piece. A lot of the guys who don't have a strong set of punching skills can take advantage of other gifts they have such as mental attributes and approach.

Q: What would you say to the critics who labeled the UFC, "Human cockfighting"?
Randy Couture: I think it's antiquated, thinking like this; they need to look at our track record, this statement is coming from a very uneducated perspective, from those who think it's just a blood sport and a bunch of thugs. Many fighters come from very respected and talented backgrounds. In this sport, it requires a lot of training and sacrifices, they need to tune in and come and look at what's really going on.

Q: UFC is making a mark in the mainstream. What are your opinions on UFC versus boxing?
Randy Couture: Not just UFC but the sport of mixed martial arts. UFC is only part of it and to put the sport in a position where it can be more mainstream, there is still a long away to go. I haven't seen anything that big sponsorship wise in mixed martial arts but one show is going on one of the major networks in the United States but no major corporate sponsorships for the athletes. It's come a long way and the pay-per-view is doing very well now, but there is a long way to go in comparison to

boxing, there are some differences. Everybody wants to compare it to boxing; boxing has its base and UFC and mixed martial arts has one as well.

Q: Why do you think boxers have been considered as the toughest men on the planet whilst Olympic amateur wrestlers never got the same level of respect and financial rewards as them?
Randy Couture: Well it's like comparing apples to oranges; wrestlers don't have a professional outlet for the sport. Professional wrestling, as everybody knows, is entertainment, it's not a real sport. Boxing, both at amateur and professional level is a sport, and mixed martial arts is a sport. Olympic and amateur wrestling has no real outlet. You can see more and more Olympic wrestlers making a transition into professional mixed martial arts.

I don't think you can say that the heavyweight champion of the world in boxing is the toughest guy on the planet anymore. That used to be the case, but not anymore. In an open fight, in a free fight, where you're not looking at rules, where you're not talking about boxing rules, it's a completely different game. Boxers don't have experience in no-rules type of fights, whereas mixed martial artists do.

Q: You are one of the few guys fighting in your forties, what keeps you going?
Randy Couture: What keeps me going is, I'm very passionate about the sport; it's what I love to do, and as long as I'm still capable of doing it, I don't see why I should do anything else. And I'm getting paid for it... I'll keep training.

Q: How do you see the future of the fastest growing sport in the world?
Randy Couture: I think it's going to continue to grow. The last generation before this was the boxing generation, last

generation wanted to watch the superstars in boxing, but this generation wants to see mixed martial artists.

Q: Am I right in saying you made a transition into Hollywood. Tell me more about the new Scorpion King movie...

Randy Couture: It's the prequel to the 'Scorpion King', the Rock is not in the movie but it's the Rock's character as a boy growing up. Rock wasn't actually involved in the movie. I'm the main bad guy in the movie and it was a lot of fun to work on it. It was really great shooting in South Africa; we were there for six weeks with Universal Pictures. The director of the film was Russell Mulcahy, who worked on such films as 'Resident Evil' - he was great to work with. I think you'll like the movie.

Q: Presently what projects are you working on; I understand you recently released a book?

Randy Couture: I'm waiting on a couple of projects, a possible two-hour pilot, a popular action drama and a couple of other movie project offers. The autobiography is basically experiences in my life; I hope it's positive, we're all given a lot of challenges in life and adversity and find a way to be successful. I have a passion in what I do and I'm very happy that the book came out. I hope people like it.

Q: Why did you leave the UFC for a while before making a return?

Randy Couture: It was never anything to do with any other organisations. Basically it was a phase in my career where I had to make the decision to fight and that made the right sense to me; like fighting Fedor [Emelianenko] who is the best heavyweight in the world. I would love to compete again but the UFC, unfortunately, can't make that fight happen.

Q: Should the UFC be paying the fighters a lot more money

than they currently are?

Randy Couture: Yes, not just in the UFC but mixed martial artists in general should be getting paid better across the board in other organisations. The top boxers are making 20, 40 million dollars for a fight. On the other hand, the top mixed martial artist in the UFC makes $500,000 per fight. As one of the top fighters, I'm certainly not complaining; the money I've made in the sport has been a great way to earn and make a living. But, at the same time, compared to other professional sports, it's paying low level compared to other professional athletes.

Q: Anything you would like to add?

Randy Couture: People can check out the training we provide at Extreme Couture. I hope to be fighting hopefully at the end of the year, where and when I don't know yet. I'm at the point of my career where I have to take fights that are right and for me. Fedor, who is one of the two best heavy weights in the world, and that's the guy I would like to compete against, but unfortunately the UFC can't make that fight happen.

MATT HUGHES

Matt Hughes has been widely known as the most dominant UFC champion in the history of the organisation. Born in Hillsboro, Illinois, like many UFC fighters, Hughes has a strong amateur wrestling background; he is a four-time collegiate all-time American champion.

Before entering the UFC, Hughes fought in smaller MMA shows, and also competed in ADCC tournament in the Middle East. Hughes made his UFC debut on 16th of December 2000, eventually becoming the UFC Welterweight champion on November 2001 when he beat Carlos Newton. Hughes went on to dominate his division in brutal fashion.

Hughes has fought some of the top names in the welterweight division, including BJ Penn, Georges St Pierre, Sean Sherk and Royce Gracie. In 2005, Hughes was the coach opposite Rich Franklin in the second season of the popular 'The Ultimate Fighter ' series, and got the opportunity once again on series six opposite former welterweight champion Matt Serra. Hughes now spends his time on his farm and coaching at the new H.I.T Squad Gym, in Granite, Illinois.

Q: Let's talk about your childhood. Did you have a normal upbringing?

Matt Hughes: I grew up on a farm with a twin brother, miles away from anybody else. I didn't have a whole lot of friends growing up; my sole friend was my twin brother. I grew up with a hard work ethic and had somebody to play with, that being my brother. When we got older, that play turned into competition, so this gave me a deep sense of competition instilled in my body. Those are two of the factors why I've been successful and competitive as I am today, because of the hard work ethic and my twin brother I was always competing with.

Q: You have a pretty strong amateur wrestling background, when and how did you get involved?

Matt Hughes: I started wrestling actually in junior high. We had wrestling in school in the P.E. period. Then we had a wrestling tournament at that end of that, so it wasn't formal wrestling, but my first formal wrestling would have been freshman in high school. I did well; then I ended up winning my state tournament in my junior and senior year. I wrestled in college and was a 4-times collegiate all-time American, and when I got this in college I still wanted to compete.

Q: When did you first hear about the UFC?

Matt Hughes: The first time I saw the UFC it was on a video tape. I forget which UFC it was, but I think it was number 3 or 4. It was when Royce Gracie choked out Dan Severn. That was the first time I watched a UFC. My brother and I watched that together.

Q: What was your reaction and did it ever occur to you at that point you may want to be part of this one day?

Matt Hughes: I didn't know if I was going to be part of the UFC in the future. I did look at Royce Gracie and thought I could physically beat him, but at the time I was watching those tapes, he definitely would have killed me because I didn't know any submission holds whatsoever, or any defence to them. So he would have killed me at the time. It's just amazing, he's the first guy I really watched and I ended up fighting him 12 years later.

Q: Tell me about your early MMA fights before you ever competed in the UFC?
Matt Hughes: I started out in a show called 'Extreme Challenge' and my first fights were extremely easy. The first lasted 30 seconds, the second lasted 45 seconds, my wrestling was really superior to everyone else's. I took people down quick, and when I got on the ground I was too athletical for my opponents. I found them very easy. I did receive a few other offers so I continued to do the same thing, and I just worked out regularly for a couple of years in a row.

Q: Did you feel you had to adapt to new training methods and not merely rely on your wrestling in the cage?
Matt Hughes: I always trained in a way where I was covering different types of training, to get better in every area. I had nothing much new to really learn, It's just the way I was - well rounded in all areas. When I first got into the MMA sport I realised you had to be as well rounded as you can be, and this will work to your benefit when you're fighting.

Q: What motivates you to put your life on the line in the cage?
Matt Hughes: The reason I go in there is because I love to compete, behind that, is that I'm good at it. I seem to do what I'm good at, and also that's my living, that's what I do, I put food on the table, clothes on my kids back, by competing in the octagon.

Q: How did you make the transition into the UFC and tell me about the fight with Frank Trigg?

Matt Hughes: Making the transition into the UFC was pretty easy, the rules were a lot like the earlier MMA events I had fought in. I had faced some tough guys before I entered the UFC, so when I did get into the UFC, I definitely was ready for that organisation and the competition level they had. So it was an easy transition. The only thing that was different was the fact there were cameras on you in the UFC, people are watching on pay-per-view, that's the big difference.

The nerves were kind of working against me because everyone's watching. With the Frank Trigg fight, I had fought him before and beat him, so this was the second fight. One thing about Frank Trigg is that he's not shy about running his mouth. He, of course, ran his mouth before this second fight and this got under my skin. Then before the fight started, the referee got us in the centre of the octagon and he tried to kind of kiss me, and I pushed him away. It was then when the final works really started for us.

Right after the fight started, I had him up against the fence, he threw a knee, and there's no doubt he felt my cup on his knee and he knew it was a low blow. I turned away and put my hands across Frank's face and I looked to the ref, [Mario] Yamasaki, and he knew nothing about the foul. Frank continued throwing punches, got me down and had me knocked out.

When I regained consciousness I could see he was on top of me, and the first thing that came into my mind was I was in a bad situation. For every move there is a counter and for every counter there is a counter. So I knew there was a way out. I took a deep breath and tried to think of ways to get out. I ended up getting out and on top of Frank, and proceeded to beat him up until he tapped out.

Q: You have fought some tough fighters, which would you say was the toughest fight?
Matt Hughes: My toughest fight was against BJ Penn, when I fought him the second time, because he beat me the first time.

That was a really stressful fight.

Q: What diet do you follow as a UFC fighter and athlete?
Matt Hughes: It just depends on what I've got going on; right now, I'll eat whatever I want. But when I'm training for a fight I get stricter with my diet. I'll eat a lot of good carbs and protein, I try to stay away from fat and I love fruit, I can eat fruit as a dessert, to be honest.

Q: How important is recuperation for a UFC fighter like yourself?
Matt Hughes: I think recuperation is a big thing, you can't be in this game as long as I have been because when you are fighting you need to take time off. So you're not beating your body up constantly. I know some guys who, all they do is train and the same way all year long, and they are not in the sport anymore. You just can't take the bumps and bruises all the time. I think, after a fight I always take quite a bit of time off and that is all relevant to who else from gym is fighting. If someone like Robbie Lawler has a fight coming up then I will get back in the gym and help him get ready for the fight.

Q: How do you see the UFC and MMA growing and getting even bigger as a sport than it already is?
Matt Hughes: We're not covered day to day on ESPN yet, so that definitely would be great for us, everyday coverage ESPN, getting on more TV shows. The more adults see us the more chance we have gaining new fans. That can all be good for the sport. All in all I'm really happy with the progress of the sport. If you look back five or six years ago and compare it with now, you'll find it's a whole new world.

Q: You fought GSP at UFC 79 and did not perform to the best of your abilities; you actually looked out of shape. What are your comments on this fight?

Matt Hughes: Of course I could have done things differently, the fight didn't go the way I wanted it to, and when that happens obviously there could have been some changes. But that's the way it is, and if we meet up and fight again then I'll have to look at things, the way I fought and how he fought and we'll come up with a different game plan. When you lose you have to look back at what I did well and what I shouldn't have done, and what I'm going to do the next time. Watching tapes of your opponent definitely helps, you look at tendencies at what they do and what they don't, and then you try to base your game plan on that.

Q: How did your fight with Royce Gracie materialise? This fight broke pay-per-view records at the time...
Matt Hughes: I don't know if it broke pay per-view box office records and I just don't care about stuff like that. My pay cheque is the same whether two people pay for pay-per-view or two million. It's just not a concern of mine. With the Royce. Gracie fight, Dana White called me up and said, "I've got your next opponent" and I said, "Who is it"? He said it was Royce Gracie, I asked when that's going to be. It was just that simple. Everyone thought it was a big fight but I never thought it was a big fight. I thought I would squash him like a bug just because he's been out of the sport for so long, and because of his age as well. I knew he was a one-dimensional fighter and I knew he was kind of 'old school'; the sport of grappling and striking on the ground is so much different than it used to be when he was competing.

Q: Rickson Gracie is more of a physical specimen; how do you think he would have fared in the UFC?
Matt Hughes: I think Rickson would get killed in the UFC, to be honest. From what I've seen in Rickson's fights, I've never been impressed by him. I just think they've made Rickson to be some fairy tale; he's just not what the rumours say he is. I really

don't think Rickson would be able to compete in the UFC.

Q: What has been the most enjoyable experience for you in your career?
Matt Hughes: I think the most enjoyable thing that's happened in the UFC for me is the good times I've had, a lot of memories, and a lot of that has to do with my family - the people I keep next to me. So this is what I will take away from what I've done in the UFC, first and foremost.

Q: Do you think TUFseries gave the UFC and MMA in general wider exposure which otherwise may not have?
Matt Hughes: I definitely think 'The Ultimate Fighter' was good for the UFC .This is one of the things which put the UFC where it is today. It got fights on Spike TV which is big, it has drama in their which attracted fans and it's just been great for the UFC. Take 'The Ultimate Fighter' out of the equation and the UFC wouldn't be where it is today.

Q: You were on the same series with Matt Serra. Were there any interesting stories behind the scenes?
Matt Hughes: Actually I don't have any interesting stories because I never talked to him. When he walked into the room I didn't take interest in whatever he was doing, whether he was talking, walking around, I didn't pay any attention to him, nor did I chat with him. So I really wouldn't have any interesting stories.

Q: Your book made it to the New York Times bestseller list and was one of the first autobiographies of a UFC star. How did the book deal come about?
Matt Hughes: The book came about because I had a lot of people asking me questions about my life, and how I was raised and got into the sport. Then I was approached by a company 'Simon Schuster' to write a book, so with those two together, I

said yes. To be honest, I didn't really want to, but I wouldn't say I was talked into it. I thought it was the right thing to do, so I went ahead and did a book deal.

Q: Do you feel amateur wrestlers - after they graduate - don't have an avenue to make money unless they pursue pro wrestling. Is the UFC a good outlet for them?
Matt Hughes: I think it's an easy cross over for a wrestler to come into this sport. I think the wrestlers have a real advantage in the fighting game in that wrestlers get to decide where the fight's going to be at. If he wants to be offensive he can take somebody down and try to beat him down. On the other hand, if he wants to be defensive, he can keep the opponent standing and try to beat him standing. So a wrestler gets to decide where the fights going to be at.

Q: In your opinion how would a heavyweight boxer do in a no rules fight?
Matt Hughes: Well, it would just depend on what the match up would be. If a heavyweight boxer comes into the UFC and fights another stand up artist who doesn't have any takedowns then maybe he'd have a chance. If that heavyweight boxer comes up against someone who has good takedowns then that boxer wouldn't really do that well. Everybody who has good hands is going to have that punchers chance, no doubt about that. But like you said, you have to be well rounded and somebody not well rounded is going to be taken weakest game and the boxer would be at a disadvantage. I really don't follow boxing, never really followed boxing as a sport, to me boxing is pretty boring; it's just two guys trying to punch each other and that's about it.

Q: Who are your favourite UFC fighters?
Matt Hughes: I'm a big Chuck Liddell fan, Rich Franklin fan, both are personal friends of mine. I always like to watch

[Thierry] Sokoudjou fight to be honest, that's my list.

Q: You have at least one more fight left in you who would this fight be against?
Matt Hughes: I think I would be fighting Matt Serra, because that fight has never taken place, but I don't know one hundred percent when that fight will happen or anything yet. But that's who I think I would be fighting.

Q: If you were not a UFC fighter what avenues would you have taken in life?
Matt Hughes: If I wasn't a fighter I would probably be working on a farm, possibly my farm, doing something with my hands, because I like using my hands whether its construction or some kind of electrical. It would definitely be something where I'm able to use my hands.

Q: Future plans once you finish fighting?
Matt Hughes: I want to spend more time with my family, that's why I would look into getting out of the fighting now. I have a 3-year old daughter who I don't spend much time with. That's the big reason. I do have a gym in Illinois called 'The Hit Squad' and we do have dormitory rooms set up so that people can train and live here.

CHUCK LIDDELL
'THE ICEMAN'

Chuck Liddell is one of the biggest names in the UFC. His trademark Mohawk hairstyle is recognisable all over the globe. Born and raised in California, Liddell started training in martial arts at the age of 12.

Liddell has become the face of the UFC and one of the major stars to propel himself into the mainstream. A quietly spoken man of very few words and a down to earth attitude, Liddell has accumulated a legion of fans where ever he has been.

His victories over such 'Heavyweights' Tito Ortiz, Randy Couture and Wanderlei Silva cemented his position as one of the all time greats in the sport of mixed martial arts. He has held the UFC light heavyweight title and has been a major force in the division having fought some of the best fighters out there and was the first UFC fighter to be on the cover of ESPN sports magazine in May 2007.

Q: Chuck, let's talk about your childhood when you were growing up in Santa Barbara!

Chuck Liddell: My mom raised us as a single-parent and did a great job. Growing up I loved sports. I played football, baseball and wrestled at San Marcos High School. We lived with my grandparents and I loved it. My Pops taught me everything I know about loyalty and honour. I had a great family with my grandfather and grandmother helped us and it was really good.

Q: How far did you get in wrestling?

Chuck Liddell: I got into wrestling when my high school football coach asked me if I wanted to wrestle, it was great and I did pretty well. My junior and senior year I finished in the top 5 at the CIF Tournament and ended up wrestling at Cal Poly in college all four years. I was a decent wrestler.

Q: Were you studying any martial arts or boxing at the time?

Chuck Liddell: When I was 12, I was watching Kung Fu Theatre actually and got interested in martial arts and started karate at 12. By chance I signed up at Koei-Kan Karate-Do. It was ran by Jack Sabat and that style of karate was perfect for me. It was still about discipline and concentration, but was combative and I have always liked that. I was a gym rat, I couldn't get enough sparring. After college, my college buddy introduced me to a gym that taught Muay Thai boxing and from there I started MMA 12 years ago.

Q: Were you ever influenced by Bruce Lee?

Chuck Liddell: I used to watch him and thought his philosophy on fighting was right on, 'use whatever's best for you' take from different styles don't just stick to one style. I definitely think he would have evolved sure, that's how he felt and looked at all different martial arts and absorb what works for you.

Q: Is it alright to tell us about some your experiences

working in bars and your unique hairstyle?
Chuck Liddell: Actually I was going to a concert with my friends and had my hair shaved real short, my friends were shaving their heads and I said "There's no way I'm shaving my whole head!" So I cut it differently and I kind of liked the reaction I got. I worked for a while as a bartender and bouncer, there were instances of me having to break up fights and the boss was cool, we did a good job. There were very few incidents where I had to throw people out. We didn't have much trouble; we could get them out peacefully by talking to them. I had a really good time.

Q: When did you first hear about and see the UFC?
Chuck Liddell: I saw the first UFC with my friends and thought it was great. We checked it out and I became interested from day one. It was real fighting and it put together two things I loved and I figured I might be able to make a living at it - turned out to be true.

Q: What did you think of Royce Gracie, who was beating all these bigger heavier guys?
Chuck Liddell: I think he did a good job in introducing Brazilian Jiu-Jitsu to everyone, now everybody is learning it.

Q: How did you pursue your dream of competing in the UFC?
Chuck Liddell: I had competed in Division 1 wrestling, karate and kickboxing. This guy who promoted kickboxing shows who knew I could wrestle asked if I wanted to fight (UFC) and to send in a tape. UFC 17 was the first one I fought in. I fought Noe Hernandez and won by decision. A friend of mine called me up and said, "You guys should get a manager, he's good and he'll be good for you!" So Dana White became my manager and it just all worked out well. I used to spar with Tito when I had a fight coming up.

Q: What feelings do you encounter when stepping into the

octagon? Do you feel fear and feel you are putting your life on the line?

Chuck Liddell: No. I get excited walking out no matter what. I love having the crowd and love that roar when I walk out. When they close the cage it's just about me and the other guy.

Q: Let's talk about some of your most memorable fights with Tito Ortiz and would you fight him again?

Chuck Liddell: It was fun. I finally could show people that I could beat him like I always said I could - and it was good to shut him up! But he is always going to be one of those that runs his mouth. I don't like that kind of thing; he talks a lot, a lot of times he's not willing to fight some guys. You have to fight anyone and not try to dodge anyone or pick or chose fighters you want to fight. I've already had the fight and beat him so I don't know why anybody would want to see the fight again. But if he came about and he came on from a winning streak and give the people and media a reasonable fight then yes, sure.

Q: What about fighting Randy Couture?

Chuck Liddell: I lost the first one and it was great to avenge in the second one and the third one was to prove it wasn't a fluke that I beat him. He is a great champion. When I fought him the second time I knew I had him because he looked tired for the first couple of minutes. It definitely helped beating him; I've always fought the toughest fighters I can get, I try to fight all the tough fighters and not dodge anybody that wants to fight me.

Q: You are one of the few non-grapplers to really do well in the UFC when nearly all the champs tend to have a very strong grappling base. What is your opinion on this?

Chuck Liddell: I am a striker with a strong wrestling base. I am very hard to take down but I have always been really good at taking people down. That was usually my strategy in college. Take the guy down.

Q: Can you highlight your training routine before a fight?
Chuck Liddell: I train twice or three times a day five days a week. I have a great team at 'The Pit'. They know how to get me ready for a fight. We work on everything, from wrestling, striking and conditioning and I train hard. I don't party before I have a fight coming up, actually I have a hard time as I go out, but I drink water and hanging out with my friends. I'm at home and with my camp. When I'm at home and not out and about two or three weeks before the fight , I'm asleep at 10 at night. When I'm out I'm out till 2 or 3 in the morning.

Q: You went onto fight in Japan for the Pride organisation can you tell us about any of your fights and the experiences there?
Chuck Liddell: I wasn't there long, but it was good.

Q: Your epic fight with Wanderlei Silva was a great victory which once again proved your ability to beat the best MMA fighters. What was it like to fight this exceptionally all round tough opponent?
Chuck Liddell: It was a fight that I had waited a long time for. I would have liked the knock out but it was still sweet. It was a great fight for the fans.

Q: Kimbo Slice is making a name in the MMA world do you think the promoters are trying to hype up a street brawler?
Chuck Liddell: He's not very well trained; the hype of him is from his record from his Youtube fights on the streets. He's just not good; the people he's fought are not very good, there's nothing impressive. He's not fought any one impressive. He's training with Bass [Rutten] right now who is working him. If they want to hype him up then let them, he's doing the right thing trying to learn to be a cage fighter and working on it.

Q: Your new book hit the New York Times bestseller list -

can you shed some light on why the fans are intrigued about MMA?

Chuck Liddell: It is a great sport and more people are realising how many things it brings together. It isn't just boxing or wrestling. In MMA fighting is real. The training is tough. These days, young kids are training in MMA and they are going to do amazing things.

Q: Do you feel UFC and its fighters have at last been embraced by the fans and respected the way boxing has been for decades?

Chuck Liddell: By fans, yes. I think it's more exciting and more things can happen in a fight, many ways to win and may different ways to lose, it makes it a much more exciting fight. I like boxing, but it's not the same for me. Our sport includes boxing but a lot more things you have to learn, boxing is limited. Doing interviews I try to explain to people and fans what the sport is all about, do autograph signing and get out and talk to fans. I like the sport, I love the sport and what I do and make sure I'll be doing it. I think it's been a great reaction from the fans.

Q: What are your plans for the future?

Chuck Liddell: To fight. I plan to fight as long as I can and my body holds up. I love fighting and I have plenty of fight left in me. I think I have about two to four years left and I hope in this time I'll be doing the same thing, I'll keep on fighting as long as my body will let me. I'm not complaining, I'm making the kind of money that we'd never had made otherwise. Dana has helped the sport grow and few might have turned against him because he's making so much money, he takes care of the fighters as far as I know. I like to spend time with my kids and spend some time seeing business side of things.

MATT SERRA
'THE TERROR'

Matt Serra is a former UFC welterweight champion who began studying martial arts at a very young age. Born to an Italian-American family in New York, Serra began studying Brazilian Jiu-Jitsu under Renzo Gracie in the 90's and competed in various tournaments. His victories included beating one of the top grapplers in the world Jean-Jacques Machado in the ADCC Submission wrestling world championship in Abu Dhabi.

He made his UFC debut on 4th May 2001 losing to Shonie Carter. However, Serra continued fighting in the UFC and has some impressive wins to his name. He was chosen to feature opposite Matt Hughes on season 6 of 'The Ultimate Fighter' series. On April 7, 2007 Serra fought Georges St Pierre to win the welterweight championship title, but lost the title on April 19, the following year to GSP in UFC 83 in Canada. Serra, who has two Brazilian Jiu-Jitsu gyms in the New York area, continues to fight in the UFC and is very well known for his rivalry with Matt Hughes.

Q: Matt, when did you get involved in the martial arts?

Matt Serra: My father is a long time martial artist and he started me off with the Wing Chun kung fu system. There was a lot of pad work involved and we did combat drills as far as training goes. I started at an early age as a kid, till when I was in high school. But then I found out whenever I got into a real altercation - which happened often with me as a kid growing up - I ended up using what I had from my training and would wrestle the guy down and did a lot of ground stuff just because it was second nature I guess. It was just natural to me.

Then my father showed me the tapes of the 'Gracies' when I was a senior in high school. It was the 'Gracies In Action' tapes which had the Gracie family fighting all these other martial arts exponents. I was very intrigued by it, then I saw the 'In Action 2' tape and I thought to myself, "I don't want my arm broken - I've got to learn this martial art!" So, soon I hooked up with Renzo Gracie and moved to Manhattan and took it right from there. He took me under his wing.

Q: Can you describe your training and experiences with Renzo?

Matt Serra: Renzo is family to me. I was working in security and bouncing on the weekends just so I could train with Renzo in Manhattan, which was a 45 minute train ride from Long Island in New York where I'm from. He saw I was tired in class sometimes not training to the best of my ability so he told me to quit that night job and just work doing some private lessons in the gym. He took me out of that situation and took me under his wing. Whenever he went to compete in Japan and he'd ring me. He went to watch me in the Pan-American games where I got a gold medal and he was my mentor and a great instructor. I owe a lot to him, so no matter how far I get or go I never surpass my instructor because Renzo Gracie really changed my life.

Q: Speaking of the Gracies what did you think of Royce, was he an inspiration in anyway?
Matt Serra: Obviously, I was just about fascinated like everybody else watching Royce fighting in the UFC. I was a fan before I became a participant in the UFC. Watching him beat those much larger guys using jiu-jitsu techniques I was totally blown away by this jiu-jitsu. I had to learn that system and thought this was just phenomenal; this art was something we've not seen before.

Q: How did you get involved in the UFC?
Matt Serra: I made a name for myself on the grappling circuit, I won the Pan-American games in purple belt in Miami, I also got a gold medal the same year in the brown belt division in the Mundials in Brazil. I also went to Abu Dhabi in the Middle East and competed in some high profile grappling matches beating some big names in the mixed martial arts and grappling world. With that along with my team mate Ricardo Almeida, the UFC stopped by Renzo's academy in Manhattan and they wanted Ricardo and me to fight in the UFC. I'm like "I'll do it". In my first UFC fight I fought Shonie Carter and lost this fight, but it gained me some experience and taught me something. That's how I got involved in it, man.

Q: Let's talk about your victory over none other than GSP when you won the belt.
Matt Serra: That was great. Before that fight I got a little more respect for my power as far as my punching power and striking ability goes. Before that I was pretty much known as a jiu-jitsu guy. People knew me as a guy who trains with the Gracie's and I was a name in grappling. So people kind of avoided going to the floor with me. No one really gave thought to my stand up game so I knew I had the elements of surprise going in and sure enough I got the right sparring partner, Ray Longo, who is my striking and conditioning coach and we had a great game plan.

We worked the body and to the head, it's always like just another day of sparring it actually worked out to be a little easier, but that's great. It was an indescribable moment when I won the title; it was just such a great feeling. It was almost surreal. I was thinking, "Look at me now". It was unbelievable and a dream come true which may sound very clichéd but it was really a dream come true.

Q: How did you get involved in TUF series?
Matt Serra: I had lost to Karo Parisyan. I had a knee injury after that loss and I had to rest a little bit. I got a call may be 11 months after that but I figured I'd be back in the UFC anyway because me and Karo had put an exciting fight. The UFC called me up and said they were doing something called 'The combat show.' I'm like, "Man, where do I sign up?" I went to an audition and next thing I'm on season 4 on 'The Ultimate Fighter' along with another veteran including 'Mr Flashy', Shonie Carter.

Q: Let's talk about Matt Hughes, behind the scenes on TUF...
Matt Serra: In the beginning he tried to be really nice, but not nice - like a nice guy type, almost like an asshole kind of condescending type. Later on behind the scenes it was, "He's just a dweeb I can't stand the guy! The guy is really not a good person. I can't wait to fight the guy because I think he's a total ass." If some people win enough fights their real personality comes out, in his case, he's arrogant - or some people like him, just don't think, he's just a stuck up jock.

He's the type of guy that bullies people in high school, he's that guy. We pretty much ignored each other. As a fighter he's very dangerous and good at what he does, if he gets you down he's very good on the top. He is a very good fighter and deserves to be in the Hall of Fame, but that doesn't mean he's a good person or I can't exploit the holes in his game. I feel I'm a complete fighter than him, I proved to him I'm a better coach, he can't say his guy won the whole thing because that guy had 30 fights going in there, I took guys who had a few fights and took them further.

I feel like I'm a way better coach than he is and I want to fight him to show him I'm a better fighter. It's not just about being big and broad, there's something called 'technique'.

Q: If the fight finally happens, how would you prepare yourself in the run up?

Matt Serra: I have to be in phenomenal shape, I told the UFC I need three months, no less. There will be no secrets, I will be looking for his chin; on the floor, I'll be looking to take a leg. If I have it my way, I'll be the nail in his coffin.

Q: Were you ever influenced by the legendary Bruce Lee?

Matt Serra: I love Bruce Lee! When I was young, kids were playing baseball but I was watching Kung Fu Theatre with my old man. I love Bruce Lee and his movies, 'Enter the Dragon',' Game of Death,' 'Return of the Dragon'. He was one of the first mixed martial artists if you ask me. He was doing arm locks in there, everything; I think it was awesome.

Q: Who is your favourite UFC fighter?

Matt Serra: Not so much in the UFC, but Renzo Gracie for the obvious reason, he's a major influence on me in and out of the cage or ring. Other than that, Royce Gracie - who is a pioneer - and Rickson Gracie too. I'm a fan of anybody who shows skills, anybody who steps in there deserves credit. It takes balls to step in the cage but it's hard to stay in there whether things are going your way or not. There's guys like [Antonio] Minotauro [Nogueira], Randy Couture, these guys are great champions and fighters. Chuck Liddell, even if it's not their fighting style I love. I like guys that are tough, they beat a guy down and they get beat down but they come back and go back in there for more; that's what I respect.

Q: Could you have performed better in the second outing against Georges St Pierre?

Matt Serra: Obviously! [laughs] I look at it this way, sometimes you have a tough day at the office, everything after you lose a fight is going to be 20 /20 when you watching it on tape. Everything's, "I should've, I could've, I would've". I'm just going to leave it at that. He was the better man on the night and I'm not about to make excuses.

Q: Is it true that you get your training and sparring partners to 'boo' you to psych you up before a fight?

Matt Serra: I said that in an interview as a joke. I said my trainer boos me all the time and what not, but that was just a joke. To tell you the truth, what I do is I watch a lot of Tim Sylvia fights and any time that jerk walks out everybody boos him. So I'm like, "Hey, he can still fight so I can do it, no big deal". I'm not a big fan of his, he's a dickhead!

Q: When you were promoting the UFC with Dana White on Fox TVone presenterwas debating with you saying MMA is not good for kids. What are your views on this rather controversial subject?

Matt Serra: Do I think little kids should fight in a cage? No! Do I think they should be studying martial arts or mixed martial arts? Yes! It's self-defence. I disagree with EliteXC who are trying to make a spectacle of Kimbo Slice, and I don't want to knock him, he's trying to make money and that's fine, but the promoters that are hyping up this internet sensation.

Now, as a result, you are going to get a bunch of moron kids with camcorders trying to be in the UFC by fighting each other in the backyard, that's not the proper way to do it. Anybody can fight any body in the street; you should come up the right way get involved in the sport, get involved in wrestling, jiu-jitsu, boxing, Thai boxing - get involved in those kind of matches. Then this will hone your skills and you will be ready to fight competitors, not on the street looking to make a name that way.

When No Holds Barred started, it wasn't a sport, before it was a freak show. Now they are doing the right thing and it's legal, legal in 33 states in the U.S. - but on the other hand, that wouldn't have been if it didn't start off in the beginning like it did.

Q: Can you recall your experiences bouncing and how do you differentiate between street fighting and MMA?

Matt Serra: There's a huge difference. I mean it's easy to fight guys that don't know what they are doing, that's one thing. You can beat up any knucklehead in the street and feel like you're superman, but when you train and you go up against the other guy who trains that's good, even if you're going into a grappling match or boxing tournament you are fighting another skilled guy.

On the other hand you're fighting some guy on the street and sucker punch him or whatever it's not the same thing at all. I bounced at a local bar so once in a while you'd get a drunk to throw out or a guy who got rowdy and you'd put a choke on, but it wasn't a big deal, and it was short lived any way thanks to Renzo.

If there were no gloves in the UFC still, a lot of guys would get more injuries to their hands and I think it would be more of a grappling situation. Guys would get their hands busted up immediately then it would go into a jiu-jitsu match, that's how I feel. Gloves aren't huge but they are for protection for avoiding breaking hands.

Q: If you never made it as a UFC fighter what would you have been doing career-wise?

Matt Serra: I might have been screwed! Just joking! [laughs]. Thank God MMA is my favourite sport. I don't know, man, I may have taught and taken that route. But like I said, I'm living the dream, thank God MMA came about and I tried Brazilian

Jiu-Jitsu. If MMA didn't come about then I'd probably still be doing Brazilian Jiu-Jitsu, I would be involved in the martial arts one way or another.

Q: What is your biggest achievement so far?
Matt Serra: Aaah! I want you to guess that one. What do you think?

Q: I think it's winning the belt.
Matt Serra: Yes it would have to be the belt, UFC welterweight belt. The other thing is I won the Pan-Americans and international competitions. Another thing I'm proud of is the match I won against Jeans-Jacques Machado, who was a legend in the jiu-jitsu world - but there's nothing that takes the place the fight with GSP, when I won the belt this was the icing on the cake. If I retire tomorrow, I know I was the champion.

Q: Have you experienced a change in the UFC since it has filtered into the mainstream?
Matt Serra: Yes, you know what, I've seen both worlds because I was fighting in 2001, when no one knows you, when you're walking around other than hardcore fans, once in a while. Or on the week of the fight it kind of feels like being a celebrity because all fans are around, all taking pictures and you feel a celebrity for a week. But now you get the same thing when you go to the 7/11 store, the super market, the movie theatre. I'm kind of getting it every time now which is a positive thing, it's good. Everybody's cool, it's a nice thing, I'm not going to be the guy complaining about it.

I didn't come off the television show, 'The Ultimate Fighter', like I said, I fought before and after the TV show. I'm not the guy who just came on 'The Ultimate Fighter' and made my name. I was fighting before that and know what it was like before the mainstream explosion. Boxing is really a dying sport, the days of Tyson are over; it's not just as exciting. There are only so many ways to win and lose in boxing, that's why UFC has taken off. I'm just not saying that because I'm a participant, but as a fan. I was a fan before I got into it and I'll be a fan when I'm out of it. I love to fight, when I have a fight coming up I'm excited whether its mine or someone else's.

Q: What are your plans for the future after you retire from competing in the octagon?
Matt Serra: Right now I just got back into training from my injury which occurred in the GSP fight. I'm getting into good shape and fighting Matt Hughes hopefully soon. I'm hoping this will happen. He wants the fight and I want the fight, and I'm coming for him. There's nothing I wanted more from a fight than this fight, and I'm coming for him this time and I can't wait. I think this is going to be a fight which is going to surpass my first fight with GSP as my favourite.

I'm going to keep on fighting, it depends on how the body holds up but right now I feel great. I own two Brazilian Jiu-Jitsu schools in Long Island, New York [www. Serrajitustu.com] I want to be teaching way long after I finish fighting because I love teaching, this is what I do. That's why I couldn't talk to you earlier because I was teaching two classes. I like bringing other fighters in mixed martial arts, so I'll be a trainer, coach and a teacher way after I finish fighting and that's going to be my life. I could just retire and teach right now, but I love to fight.

MARK COLEMAN
'THE HAMMER'

Mark 'The Hammer' Coleman was the first fighter to be officially crowned UFC heavyweight champion and he was inducted into the UFC Hall of Fame in March 2008. Coleman began freestyle Olympic wrestling as a teenager, and was a two-time mid-American Wrestling Conference champion; he won a NCAA championship and was awarded a spot on the American Olympic team.

As a kid growing up, Coleman's interests leaned towards sports and his desire was to become an Olympic wrestling champion or a top football player. Coleman made his UFC debut in 1996 at UFC 10, and fought for the organisation for 3 years, before making the transition to Pride. He quickly grabbed the attention of the Japanese fans as he smashed his way to victory in the ground-breaking, Pride Open Weight Grand Prix in 2000. Following an up-and-down career in Japan, Coleman re-signed with the UFC in 2008, ready to take on the best heavyweights that UFC has to offer.

Coleman was principally responsible for inventing the strategy which is referred to as 'ground and pound', a simple but effective form of fighting which is now used by all MMA fighters. He is the founder of 'The Hammer House' fight team and will be remembered as one of the early UFC pioneers.

Q: Let's talk about your childhood and your freestyle wrestling career?
Mark Coleman: When I was a 5 year old kid I wanted to play all sports. American Football was very popular and so was baseball - and wrestling was in between these two sports. I loved one-on-one competition. My father was a wrestler; I wanted to be the best at everything I did sports-wise. Sports is the only thing that mattered to me, and I wanted to be the best in all three of these sports, that's how I got started as a very young boy. That's all I did;athletics.

In school education may be I didn't try so hard, I wish I would have but I did just enough to stay eligible and to be able to compete. As a young boy my goals were to be an Olympic champion or a NFL football star or major league baseball player. This is what I dreamed of when I was a little boy.

Q: Did you ever try for the Olympic team?
Mark Coleman: I became a state champion in high school and went on to college and became a national champion for Ohio State University. And after I graduated from college, I became a coach and began my preparation for trying to win a world championship and Olympic gold medal. In 1990, I became the Pan-American games gold medalist; this is when I became a National Freestyle champion, so I was ranked the number one in America in the freestyle division.

In 1991, I made the world team and finished second, losing to the Russians which made me the second ranked in the world in 1991. Now I had one more year to prepare for my ultimate goal, which was to become an Olympic Gold medalist. I made the Olympic team which was one of the biggest highlights of my life up till then. At the Olympic Games, I finished 7th place, which was very disappointing for me at the time because I was planning on winning the gold medal, of course.

Q: When did you first hear about the UFC and what was your reaction?

Mark Coleman: After the 1992 Olympics when I finished 7th place, it was the turning point of my career. In America, amateur wrestling is only important to myself, it means nothing to rest of America, because it's very hard to make a living and there's no money in the sport of amateur wrestling. And it's not very popular compared to the other sports. So I retired from wrestling, and I started seeing Ultimate Fighting on TV in 1993. I immediately knew this is what I wanted to do, but you have to get the opportunity, so in order to get a chance, I started wrestling again in 1995.

I met Kurt Angle who was the world champion in America that year, and I beat him in a wrestling match. He made the American team, and again, in 1996, I tried for the Olympic team but lost in the semi-finals. At this point, I'm 31 years old and my wrestling career is basically finished at this stage. So now I need to find a way to get into the UFC. Fortunately a manager was at the Olympic trials when I lost, he had heard about me and he knew I was interested in fighting. He approached me with a contract and asked me if I wanted to fight in the UFC in about 30 day's time. So basically, I signed a contract with this manager and I went from the Olympic trials wrestling match and walked into a cage 30 days later.

Q: When you walked into the cage did you only have Olympic Wrestling experience and some street fighting experience?

Mark Coleman: The manager knew I wanted in, and some rumours that were circulating were I had street fighting experience before. I would admit to doing a little bit of street fighting - I won all my street fights, of course. I never wanted to lose a street fight and never wanted to lose a wrestling match. To me wrestling and fighting went hand in hand. I just didn't like to lose.

Q: Being a grappler yourself what did you think of a small guy such as Royce Gracie beating much bigger, heavier and stronger guys in the UFC?

Mark Coleman: Early on, just like everybody else in America; we call it 'being dumb' or 'naive', I did not care about jiu-jitsu or stand up fighting because I knew I was going to nullify the stand up game very easily, and as for the jiu-jitsu, I never had much respect for it at the time. All we wrestlers in America always felt that in a street fight or in a cage, we were the best. In the beginning every athlete was representing their sport. I was representing wrestling and I believed the wrestlers were the toughest and the best. I had 30 days during that time and I did study the very basics of jiu-jitsu. Back in the early days what made jiu-jitsu ineffective was that head butts were legal, you can't go for an arm bar or a submission hold when somebody is able to head butt you or punch you with their left or right hand.

My game plan was very simple, that's why I came up with the phrase 'I'm gonna ground and pound him'. Now everybody uses this term, and it's a very famous term now and I was the very first to say this. It was very effective, but I must admit I was also a little lucky in the beginning because I did not face any one who had really good submission skills. This was very helpful in the beginning because may be I would have got into trouble. The head butt is the equaliser as it nullified most submission attempts.

Q: In the beginning, the grapplers were dominating the UFC; later, strikers started to do well. Is it imperative to be a complete fighter?

Mark Coleman: In the beginning some guys were much less talented than others, for sure. Obviously, nowadays fighters are well rounded. That's what I said in the beginning, the strikers will have to learn how to grapple to stand a chance in the octagon - and this is what happened; the grapplers learned how to strike as well as learning submissions.

Nowadays, you have to be black belt level in every area to be the champion. In the beginning I was fortunate that my style was effective enough to win me the title, but if you only know one style now you don't have a chance in a fight these days. The athletes now are incredibly well rounded in all areas. Now you have fighters who started out when they were 10 years old who now are 25 years old, that means they've been doing it for 15 years, obviously they're excellent in all areas. I consider them the best athletes in the world.

Q: You became the first UFC heavyweight champion by beating another legendary fighter, Dan Severn. Was this your ultimate goal, to become the heavyweight champion in the UFC?

Mark Coleman: With this fight, people had their own conception of what was going to happen. When I took my gloves off they assumed it was going to be more of a wrestling match and that I was going to trying to take him down and choke him. But my game plan for this fight was different. When I took my gloves off I knew I'd do more damage when I hit him, and I wanted to stand up and trade with Dan Severn.

He decided to take me down, which at the time in our careers, I thought I was a much better wrestler and striker than him, but when he decided to take me down he was unsuccessful, and from that point on people say that I was, maybe, kind to Dan Severn because he was a fellow wrestler. But I'll tell you this is just not true! Because once I'm in the cage it doesn't matter - I've been in the cage up against many friends before - whether they're a friend or not; they're not a friend in the cage. The reason I didn't punch Dan Severn by ground and pounding him like I did to many other fighters is because I had to take what he gave me, and what he gave me was a side head lock choke.

I don't care how I win the fight, I just finish the fight

any way I can. He gave me the side headlock choke and I took it and finished him off early and quickly. For me, this fight was incredibly great and one of the highlights of my career.

Q: Any behind the scenes UFC stories you would like to share with us?
Mark Coleman: All the fighters seem to be a lot like [each other], obviously we have a lot of differences but before a fight, and after a fight it's completely a different atmosphere. After a fight we like to drink a couple of bears and enjoy the moment, and are happy that the whole things over, win or lose, you live to see another day. I definitely had some incredible times in the last ten years of my life and I've traveled and seen the whole world.

To me, it's been an amazing experience and I met some great people in the process and had a lot of fun. Actually I've not been to the UK but I really look forward to going there. The dollars not worth shit, so someone will have to lend me a few pounds over there (laughs). The sport has grown and the U.K has accepted it. About five years ago I was supposed to fight James Thompson but the fight got cancelled a day before we were supposed to fight. I respect how far he's come along and he's a big name here right now. He's obviously paid his dues, maybe we can have that fight one day in England I hope it works out for sure.

Q: How did your career blossom in Japan?
Mark Coleman: My history over in Japan was a great experience and I had a good time. I had some real high moments with the Pride Grand Prix in which I competed in. There were some big wins for me. I became a professional wrestler in Japan with 'Hustle Hustle' and couple of other companies over there. So I got to work as a Pro wrestler which was another great experience. The fans in Japan are second to nobody because they really love the sport of mixed martial arts

and treat the fighters really well. It was unfortunate how everything had to end for Pride, but there are a couple of other companies who have started up to fill the void.

You get 50,000 people waiting to see the fights in the stadiums in Japan; someone needs to put the shows on because the fans want to watch these. I miss Japan as well, at the same time I'm very happy to be back fighting in the UFC, which was my goal all along. UFC was the first, and now it's the biggest and the strongest organisation in the world. I'm very happy they have given me the opportunity to fight again. They are the NFLof MMA and I look forward to the challenge of coming back and showing the Americans I am still fighting and I'm proud of it.

Q: Did you really stomp on Wanderlei Silva's throat after your fight in Pride 31?

Mark Coleman: No, I did not stomp on his throat. I visualised winning the fight against [Mauricio] 'Shogun' [Rua], But after the fight I thought there might be a problem with the Chute Boxe corner. Even, prior to the fight, me and the Chute Boxe team had a very good relationship. I knew if I win the fight this relationship might become sour. When I did win the fight sure enough they jumped into the ring and it was no longer a fight in the ring or cage where there is a referee, now it became a street fight.

Like I said, sometimes I do my best fighting when there's no clock and no referee, the less rules for me the better. All I had In my corner was Phil Baroni and my father, and on their side, I don't know who walked in because it happened so fast. I had a lot of people coming at me all at once so I had to move. I threw a couple of punches and finally, before he [Silva] got to me he tripped up, so he started to get my leg and we scrambled a lot and took a couple of punches.

Near the ropes, Phil Baroni and Wanderlei Silva were fighting on the ground with each other. The next thing, I was stuck up on the ropes and looked down and made eye contact with none other than Wanderlei Silva, who was down below me in a very bad position. He was looking at me, and yes I did have the opportunity to stomp on his face if I wanted to. But this is not my style, I am a fighter not a killer, so instead of stomping on his face I did put my foot on his throat just to let him know that.

This pissed him off so he started squirming really hard, and he got up back on his feet. I thought it was going to be round two but somehow they kept matters calm. I'd seen him coming and I didn't appreciate him attacking me like he did. If he didn't trip when he was coming for me he would have hit me as hard as he could in the side of the head without me looking with a sucker punch. If he had the opportunity he would have hit me.

That was the end of the evening. I was very happy because that was a very critical fight in my career because it was the last fight on my contract and I needed that win really bad. I really prepared hard for it and was very confident. The adrenaline afterwards, the whole thing about the Wanderlei incident looking back at it, is just another story to tell. It was scary and dangerous but a lot of fun. After the fight was more fun than doing the actual fight. I felt for sure they were going to create some controversy with me and the Chute Boxe team. That would have been a nice little rivalry between the Hammer House versus the Chute Boxe teams.

Q: Another one of your controversial fights was against Don Frye in the UFC. Was a man named Hamilton responsible for this mess?
Mark Coleman: I don't talk much about Hamilton because in the beginning our relationship started out good, he approached me for the Olympic trials and gave me the UFC contract. Even though the contract was very unfair, I had to pay him a lot of my money but I didn't care about that, I signed the contract. He

was also looking at Mark Kerr and Tom Erickson, all three of us, and offered us all a contract saying in 30 days we could be in the UFC.

I asked him where I needed to sign. He said, "Don't you want to read it"? I didn't care, it wasn't important to read it, I just needed the opportunity to get into this UFC tournament. I didn't want him to give it to anybody else like Mark Kerr or Tom Erickson. I don't want to call him, Mr Hamilton, his name's Rich Hamilton; whatever his name is… that's not even his real name, Rich Hamilton is not even his real name.

Anyway, he went to Tom Erickson and Mark Kerr and both of them told him that they wanted to think about it and would get back to him. I asked Rich Hamilton where I needed to sign and asked him who else he was looking at. He said Mark Kerr and Tom Erickson. I said "Listen I'm the man for the job, I'll beat Mark Kerr or Tom Erickson's ass. I'll tell you what, I'll win UFC 10, I guarantee you."

He said, "You have to be in Alabama in 2 days" and I told him I'd be there. I packed up some shit and I flew over. I had to listen to this guy trying to teach me in the ring, in the beginning I wasn't open to learning stuff from other people. In wrestling I always mostly taught myself to wrestle and I was considered not very coachable. In wrestling I was called the 'black sheep' because when most of the coaches in training sessions told me to do one thing, I would go over there and do something which was best for me instead. Maybe in hindsight I should've listened more, but I did things my way.

Now, in fighting I already had my game plan in how to I was going to win this tournament, but now I had to listen to Richard Hamilton who was trying to teach me. I didn't really want to listen to him very much, because I had my own plan. He told me Don Frye was a very bad guy – he had trained him for UFC 9 but Don Frye left him. Everybody left Richard Hamilton for a reason, we all left him for a reason; we didn't like him. I don't want to get into that but it just didn't work out.

Any way, when Don Frye left him, he told me many bad things about Don Frye to get to hate him. He told me Don had hurt people and couple of his students on purpose in practise, he told me he broke this guy's knee, messed up the other guy's ankle, and these guys actually came in clutches and then told me that Don Frye was a bad guy. So it made the fight personal. During the fight, my girlfriend and Don Frye's wife were made to sit next to each other, during the whole fight. I could hear them both screaming the whole time.

The fight went just how I planned it to go. I was a bigger, stronger wrestler than Don Frye and I was very talented, I was going to take him down and there was nothing he was going to do about it. What I didn't count on was just how much balls he had. I couldn't believe the punishment and damage he was taking. Back in those UFC's, the referee wasn't allowed to stop the fight. It was getting pretty ugly now. At one point the referee did break us up, I didn't understand why he did this because there was no stoppages back then at all. They just cleaned Don Frye up.

I think the promoters wanted Don Frye to possibly win this fight because sometimes the promoters have their favourites, of course. So they re-started the fight and the same thing happened, I took him down and I was ground and pounding him. Finally at the 11th minute mark they stopped the fight. Honestly, I was so tired myself, a lot of my friends came into the ring and crowded me. I remember it was so hot I almost passed out because I couldn't breath.

Don Frye has the biggest balls and heart in the business. We have since fought in Japan as well but it's very hard to talk about the first fight, it was a classic. We have since had respect for each other and he is considered a very good friend of mine. Richard Hamilton is a friend of neither one us.

Q: What do you think of the steroids controversy in the MMA world? Would I be right in saying your friend Mark

Kerr went through some of this?

Mark Coleman: Mark Kerr was more addicted to pain killers, if you watch the documentary he was doing pain killers. As far as steroids in MMA, I think they've done a great job with the drug testing, I don't see it as being a problem because if you cheat you are going to get caught.

Q: The UFC has now spread into the mainstream. You were fighting when the sport was being banned; what are your feelings now that you are back?

Mark Coleman: It's obviously grown into the mainstream, just look at the buy rates and the ratings on the TV, they are on the charts doing a million buys. It's grown into an incredible phenomenon in America. You have fans everywhere and I'm happy to be part still of it. The UFC announced my come back and inducted me into the Hall Of Fame which was an awesome great experience. If I just got into the Hall of Fame that would've been OK, but the UFC has also signed me to a contract and this is what I always wanted.

Now I realise how big this thing has become, the fans have treated me very well. America is the UFC country and in America they love UFC and MMA .There are all these other companies competing with the UFC but the competition is needed, and in my mind UFC is the NFL right now.

Q: What is in store for Mark Coleman?

Mark Coleman: Having restarted with the UFC, I recently signed a 4 fight deal. I was scheduled to fight Brock Lesnar on August 9th and was looking forward to this fight. This was my chance to really make an impact back in America. A lot of people were looking forward to this fight. I was training and everything was going very well, I was training hard. At the same time, in this sport any day can be your last day. During sparring I tore my ligament and basically it's going to take 6 weeks to heal up, the only good thing about it is there's no

105

surgery.

The fight's been cancelled and I'm healing my leg right now and I'm doing what I can, and when I'm a hundred percent I'll continue my training and we'll see what the UFC has in mind for me. Hopefully a rematch with Brock Lesnar or I'll fight either in the heavyweight division or drop down to 205 pounds division and maybe fight Michael Bisping.

BROCK LESNAR

Brock Lesnar grew up on a farm in South Dakota and, from humble beginnings, the physically imposing heavyweight became the most popular WWE wrestler of his generation. Before pursuing professional wrestling, Lesnar was an accomplished amateur wrestler with a number of titles under his belt. He won the 2000 NCAA [National Collegiate Athletic Association] wrestling championships in the heavyweight division. Soon after, he signed up with the WWE.

After experiencing great success in pro-wrestling, Lesnar decided to get involved in mixed martial arts, winning his debut fight against South Korean fighter Min Soo Kim by submission in June 2007. He then signed up with the UFC, losing his first match to Frank Mir. Regardless of his first loss, Lesnar is one of the few top pro wrestlers to have made a transition into the UFC and has the skills to be labeled as the 'next big thing' by many observers.

There's no doubt more pro-wrestlers may follow Lesnar into the sport of MMA as the UFC's popularity increases and pro-wrestling fans switch over to see their heroes battle for real, as opposed to the staged matches of the WWE.

Q: Brock, how would you describe your childhood?
Brock Lesnar: I grew up on a dairy farm; my childhood was like any other kid I suppose. Growing up on the farm I had a lot of work to do and not enough money to pay the bills. I wanted to wrestle in the senior Olympics when I was young, but I never had any one thing I wanted to do when I grew up. I just knew I didn't want to be a farmer though, when I grew up.

Q: How did you get into amateur wrestling and how far did you get?
Brock Lesnar: I got into amateur wrestling when I was 5 years old. My coach at the time only lived a couple of miles away from me. My parents knew him and I just started to go to wrestling classes when I was really young and I was pretty decent at it. I think when I was at 100 pounds, I won the state title. From then, I wrestled in high school and I was somewhat successful, placing third a few years in a row. When I was wrestling in junior college in Bismark, North Dakota - where my family was from - I became a heavyweight champion. Then I was recruited by the University of South Dakota and my first year there I was the finalist in the State championships and placed second in the NCCA tournament. In my senior year, I won the heavyweight championship - that was in 2000.

Q: Growing up as a teenager did you have any other interests in combat sports?
Brock Lesnar: I had interest training in boxing, but the boxing gym was 50 miles from my house. I could never get there. Friends of mine actually went to boxing but I could never afford to and never had the time to get there because of my work.

Q: Let's talk about your pro wrestling career!
Brock Lesnar: I was recruited by the World Wrestling Entertainment who had seen me win the NCCA title which was televised on ESPN. I enjoyed wrestling as a pro for a while and

after a while it became stale, so I wanted something new as I was very competitive and missed competing in real matches. I traveled a lot; being on the road every day, it was all the same. Some of my memorable matches were with Kurt Angle among others, but I enjoyed it. It was a good experience for me but after a while it became stale. It was the same thing every day and I also wanted to spend more time with my daughter.

Q: What sparked your interest to get into MMA?
Brock lesnar: I had interest to get into MMA many years ago, back in 1997, but I didn't really know how to get into it. I was living in California in 1997 training for the summer training for wrestling. Probably there was only one place I knew that had a gym that specifically trained for MMA fighting near me. I wanted to fulfill my college wrestling dream and pro wrestling, so I didn't pursue MMA back then. When I got out of amateur wrestling, MMA wasn't very huge at the time and I had a guarantee contract with pro-wrestling sitting on the table so it was easy enough for me to make the decision.

Q: I hear you were inspired by Royce Gracie, how did you hear about him?
Brock Lesnar: I watched him in the very first UFC's; he was a very petite looking human being choking people and making them submit. This was very intriguing to me. His small size and controlling people the way he did it was pretty remarkable and I thought it was very interesting. Royce Gracie is the very first guy who really made it interesting, he got into the octagon with anybody, guys weighing 300 pounds, he was the pioneer of the sport. He's been around for a long time; he was fighting and still is fighting. Later he fought in the K1 Dynamite show at the same show I made my MMA debut. This is where I met Royce for the first time.

Q: Can you describe what felt like fighting in your first

MMA fight?

Brock Lesnar: It was an excellent feeling, it was very surreal. To me, it was a great feeling to get in the ring and be competing. Before fighting in MMA I checked out Pat Miletich's gym and different people in Arizona and Indianapolis. Since I had been on the road for a long time when I was wrestling pro, it was really important for me to be at home and train and do what I always wanted to do - and that was to fight. For me to be able to come home every night and sleep in my own bed and train was a big factor in choosing a gym. I was going to train with Royce but we were never able to work a schedule out.

Q: What is the difference between the pro wrestling training you were accustomed to and the MMA training you do now?
Brock Lesnar: It's not even the same. It's like amateur wrestling training is different to pro-wrestling. Pro-wrestling is entertainment .You have to be an athlete to be in the ring; for me, training for mixed martial arts means to train in different disciplines every day - striking, kicking, jui-jitsu, elbows, Muay Thai. Pro-wrestling training is not even comparable to MMA training. Now I train one or two times a day, five or six days a week. The whole key to training is you are then able to recover and get the maximum out of it and be ready for the next day's work out, so it's beneficial to me. We train pretty hard, I have to listen to my body I'm not a spring chicken either and, day by day, week by week, the more we do, the more I can absorb and try to prepare myself when a fight's coming up.

Q: How do you feel about WWE wrestlers making a transition into the UFC, and who is your favourite UFC fighter?
Brock Lesnar: Kurt [Angle] would probably, but I think that time has come and gone already. I don't see a lot of them making the transition for the lack of amateur wrestling experience. I like watching St Pierre, but I don't have any

particular favourite UFC fighters. I like watching them all as everybody brings something different to the octagon.

Q: In your UFC debut you fought Frank Mir and actually went in real hard and had him in trouble, until he took hold of your ankle...
Brock Lesnar: I knew he would attempt to go for my legs, I got over-excited; I spent time learning how to defend and learning every discipline, so only lack of experience is the key word there for my loss. Someday, I may have a rematch with Frank but right now I have to focus on Heath Herring.

Q: Do you feel the money fighters make is sufficient or will this change in the future as the sport continues to grow and evolve?
Brock Lesnar: I hope so, for the sake of fighters.

Q: Why do you think the UFC is taking over boxing and pro-wrestling?
Brock Lesnar: It's good for the sport. UFC is new and refreshing to the people and that's what people want, something new and different and the best versus the best fighting. People want to see the best in one area against the best in another area. They are able to see this when they tune in and buy the UFC pay-per-views. The sport has evolved to what it is now and it's changed a lot of different things. Hopefully I've brought WWE fans along with me into the UFC, if you look at the ratings they speak for themselves.

Q: What is your ultimate goal in the UFC?
Brock Lesnar: I want to win the UFC heavyweight title. I appreciate everybody hanging with me. Careers come and go and can be ended very quickly. I just take one day at a time and as for future plans I don't believe I would go back into pro-wrestling.

ANTONIO NOGUEIRA
'MINOTAURO'

A ntonio 'Minotauro' Rodrigo Nogueira was born in Vitoria da Conquista, Brazil. He started his martial arts training with Judo at the tender age of 5. Later he would start training in Brazilian Jiu-Jitsu and boxing and making his MMA debut in 1999 in the 'World Extreme Fighting' event.

He competed in the RINGS promotion in Japan and won five consecutive tournament matches to claim the organisation's 'King of Kings' title in 2000. Since this historic achievement, the Brazilian has gone on the claim the Pride Fighting Championships heavyweight title, the Pride interim heavyweight title, and UFC interim heavyweight title.

After success in the land of the rising sun, Nogueira signed for the UFC and beat Heath Herring in his debut fight in UFC 73 on 2nd July 2007. On February 2nd 2008 he beat Tim Sylvia to obtain the UFC interim heavyweight title and became the first fighter to hold both the UFC and Pride heavyweight championship belts at any one time. Experts agree that Nogueira is one of the toughest fighters in the sport, a fighter known for his ability to combine technical striking and sublime submission skills.

Q: You stared martial arts training at a very young age, how and when did you get involved?

Antonio Nogueira: I stared judo at the age of 5, most of the kids in Brazil do judo to develop discipline and it's a very common and a popular sport in Brazil. I trained for 9 years, then I did Tae kwon do and some boxing. I stared doing boxing and jiu-jitsu when I was a teenager. Then in the 1990s, I started MMA and moved to America.

Q: You had an accident when you were a child, did this affect your training in any way?

Antonio Nogueira: I was 11 years old when I had a truck accident and I had a really hard time for 11 months in the hospital, I couldn't walk. I had a lot of difficulties. I was a normal kid but I couldn't do any sport after the accident for a while because of the difficulties after the accident. But I tried to get involved and had good support from my family.

Q: How popular was mixed martial arts in Brazil at the time?

Antonio Nogueira: When I was growing up, it wasn't that popular. I did a lot of different kind of martial arts, but mixed martial arts wasn't as popular as it is today. When I was 15 years old I was doing a lot of boxing and judo and also started watching the first UFC back in 1993. I was a big fan of Royce Gracie and all those guys. I started training in jiu-jitsu because of Royce Gracie's style and I had experience in boxing and judo training. That's when I thought about getting into MMA after seeing the first UFC.

Q: What were your impressions of Royce Gracie who was a small slender-looking guy beating up the bigger guys?

Antonio Nogueira: Jiu-Jitsu was the more appreciated fighting system and liked by other styles. Today we have fighters who are athletes and are big, who have good technique too. They know jiu-jitsu, wrestling and boxing. Before it was style against style, where a jiu-jitsu guy would be fighting against a karate guy, or fighting against a boxer. This showed that jiu-jitsu was the more superior martial art. I think Royce Gracie's technique was superior to all the other guys from the different martial arts and that's why I started studying jiu-jitsu.

When I saw Royce fighting, I said to myself, "I've got to do what he's doing", which was Brazilian Jiu-Jitsu which had good technique. Rickson is a good jiu-jitsu stylist, but I think his brother Royce Gracie is much better than him because he's fought the top fighters and he showed good jiu-jitsu. Rickson had his time and he's 48 years old now; he didn't fight in America, but he could've done that. But his brother did, that's why I became a professional fighter because I was watching his brother, Royce's fights. Rickson did good in Japan but I think Royce is more well known in America.

Q: Were you ever influenced by Muhammad Ali?
Antonio Nogueira: I love Ali! He did a lot of talking but he was good in his time. He helped to stamp out racism and did a real good job. He was in a sport which he used to deliver some message to the world against racism. He did a good job and he was a great athlete and that's why I like him. I'm a big fan of his.

Q: What do you think would happen if a heavyweight boxer competed in the UFC?
Antonio Nogueira: Boxing is a very different sport compared to MMA. If a boxer fights in the UFC, he has got to be prepared. I'll compare the UFC and MMA to boxing by giving you an example; you've got a normal surfer and, on the other hand, you've got a surfer who surfs in the big waves. Not many people can surf in the big waves and not many people can fight in the UFC, only the tough guys. I compare it this way; you have to train in karate, boxing, wrestling and it takes a long time

115

to get to the UFC standard. There's a lot of techniques and different things to learn, it's a very tough sport, believe me. If you have been on the top in another sport it doesn't mean you are going to be a good UFC fighter, it takes time.

Q: When did you make your MMA debut?
Antonio Nogueira: My first fight in MMA was in 1995 when I was 22 years old.

Q: Can you tell me about your success in Japan?
Antonio Nogueira: I started in Florida, in Orlando; then went to fight in Japan in 2000 in a competition called 'RINGS', which was a new tournament really growing in popularity in 2000. I had some good friends there and it was my dream to go to Japan and fight in good shows and show my technique. The Japanese love the jiu-jitsu style. So this was a stage in my life where I loved to fight over there and had my best fights of my career there. I was the Pride champion and also King of Kings champion. I had a very good time in Japan.

Q: What is the difference between the American and Japanese fans?
Antonio Nogueira: The Japanese fans understand the Jiu-Jitsu style because they have a lot of judo guys fighting there who are good on the ground, so they understand the sport technically. They know the names of the techniques and positions and this is the difference. I like to fight in both countries.

Q: When you fought Fedor Emelianenko, what problems did you encounter in the fight?
Antonio Nogueira: He's very tough; he's good at wrestling, actually he's better than me in wrestling. He threw me down and was good enough on the ground and gave me a lot of problems in the fight. Everything I tried I just could not control him. He beat me twice and one was a no contest. I hope we can

fight one more time or even 2 more times in the future. He's the toughest guy in the world and in the list of top fighters. I hope in the future I can fight him again.

Q: Your first fight in the UFC was against Heath Herring. How did you feel about fighting in the UFC?
Antonio Nogueira: Yes, this was a good fight and actually I had fought him a couple of times before in Pride, in Japan, where he was a big name before entering the UFC. I was a new fighter coming through and he had beaten some good fighters - and he was a new rising star in Japan and we had some good fights. When we fought in the UFC I was in control of the fight; I was doing good by dominating the fight standing up then he surprised me but he couldn't knock me out. I came back in the second round, where I pretty much dominated him, but he's hard to submit, he's one of the top fighters. I tried to beat him with my boxing and stand up skills, but this strategy didn't work against him. He's tough enough.

Q: Why did you make a transition to fight in the UFC?
Antonio Nogueira: When you work in a company for a while and they start to have some financial problems you decide to make decisions because they may do something different. I was waiting for what was in store for me in the future with the Japanese organisation. I didn't resign with Pride and also at the time someone asked me to come to America to make a team. In the UFC, they have big name fighters and the sport was growing so I was keeping in tune with what was happening there. I was established in Japan as a fighter and a big name. The sport was really growing in America and they were going to pay more money.

So when Dana White's offices called me, we had a conversation and then me and Dana White had a conversation and I agreed to fight for the UFC when my contract finished in Japan. Dana gave me a good proposal so I came over. I was happy and my family was already in South Florida and I had a lot of students there so I opened my own gym in Miami .So everything happened at the same time. I've got my family here in Florida and it's a good place to be right now.

Q: Do you think fighters must go to America to make it big? Even though No Holds Barred was big in Brazil, do you think the Gracie Brothers sooner or later had to come over to the U.S to really get noticed?
Antonio Nogueira: That's right! America is the centre of everything all over the world. I was big in Japan and the big main television channel in Japan was showing my fights. But if you are in America and are well known you will be well known all over the world. People take note of anything that goes on in America because there's better promotion, more events, and because of Hollywood everybody follows what the Americans are doing. That's why I felt, "When I'm in America I will be known more all over the world." When the UFC grows more in America, then they will bring the UFC to Japan and the sport's going to grow all over the world.

Q: There are a lot of Brazilians coming through the UFC right now, Anderson Silva, Wanderlei Silva and yourself, of course. Do you think more Brazilians will conquer the UFC in future?
Antonio Nogueira: I think the Brazilians are the best in this sport, because we are very traditional. Like I said, Brazil has been doing the sport for more than 60 years. We have to fight in the best place and the UFC is the biggest event in the world right now, that's why all the Brazilians are coming and looking forward to fighting in the best place.

Q: What elements of training do you incorporate when preparing for a fight?
Antonio Nogueira: I do a lot of jiu-jitsu and Muay Thai as well

as boxing. A couple of times I train wrestling including Greco Roman, about 2 times a week we spar MMA-style, integrating everything. We have to train separately Jiu-Jitsu to get good at jiu-jitsu, boxing to get good at boxing; we can't train only MMA session. You have got to have some different disciplines and two to three times a week we mix it up with hard training in MMA. I also incorporate free weight lifting to get in the best possible condition for a fight and I've been doing that a lot for 20 years now.

Q: Do you feel you are likely to dominate the UFC heavyweight division and who would you most like to fight?
Antonio Nogueira: Whoever the UFC want me to fight, I will be ready to fight that person. I will be fighting Frank Mir soon, I'm still hungry and I have a lot of things to show. I think I'll show a lot of submissions in the UFC in my future fights. I'm ready and in good shape to defend my belt and have a couple of more years yet left in me. I had a lot of tough fights in the past including against Cro crop and Bob Sapp, these were both tough fights.

Q: You beat Tim Sylvia to clinch the heavyweight title, what did you think of your opponent?
Antonio Nogueira: Tim was in very good shape and I couldn't put him down. He was very good and it was very hard to hold him and put him down, so I had to find another way to beat him. He knocked me down in the first round. I fought his game for two rounds and, when I put him in my game, we went to the ground where I finished the fight in the third round. It was a very tough match first half of the fight and at the end my technique worked.

Q: Tell me about your new venture, you recently opened a new gym in Miami with Anderson Silva?
Antonio Nogueira: We opened a gym in Miami and we have

coaches offering good training and fighters are coming through. It's the biggest MMA place in Miami and we have the most experienced coaches teaching there. So we have a good wrestling coach, a good boxing coach, a good jiu-jitsu coach and it's a great place to be training in MMA. We have a matt space of about 3000 sq ft, a cage, and professional rings. We have one of the biggest MMA teams in America. We are going to have some top fighters fighting in the UFC and at all the big events.

Q: How do you relax?
Antonio Nogueira: I like to watch movies and go to the beach in Miami. I like to spend my time in my house too, I've got dogs and I love dogs. Sometimes when I'm not fighting I like to go on my motorcycle and also I like spending time with my girlfriend. I love to eat Japanese food. I've been traveling a lot and when I'm doing seminars all over the world I like to meet different people in different countries and experience their cultures.

RASHAD EVANS
'SUGAR'

Rashad Anto Evans was born in New York, though a life in competition has seen him gravitate to New Mexico where he currently trains at the world-famous, Greg Jackson's Submission Fighting gym. Before his emergence as a top fighter in the UFC, he demonstrated some genuine wrestling skill by winning a number of titles. After wrestling throughout his studies, Rashad graduated from Michigan State where he earned a degree in psychology.

He won the heavyweight division of 'The Ultimate Fighter' 2 which aired in August 2005 and became almost a household name in the process. Evans is a charismatic fighter with a great personality whose dream has always been to fight in the UFC after being mesmerised by Royce Gracie, who was beating bigger and stronger opponents in the earlier UFCs.

Evans is one of the biggest rising stars of the organisation and his immaculate record speaks for itself. In UFC 88, he knocked out Chuck Liddell in the second round. After knocking out Chuck Liddell in spectacular fashion at UFC 88, Rashad 'Sugar' Evans will be looking to continue his career-long winning streak and aim for that coveted light-heavyweight title.

Q: Rashad, you have a fairly extensive wrestling background, can you please culminate on this?
Rashad Evans: My wrestling career started off in high school, and I did pretty good. I placed fourth in the New York State tournament, after that I went to Michigan State Community College where I placed fourth in the national tournament, and then I became the American champion the following year. I never actually trained with Dan Severn but I went to his gym and trained there, but he was never there when I was training. So I never got a chance to train with him. He's the kind of a guy who would show up from time to time.

Q: You graduated from Michigan State in Psychology. What are your thoughts on UFC fighters, as a large percentage of them are actually highly educated individuals?
Rashad Evans: I think because of the development of the sport you can't just win with lacking technical excellence. In this sport you have to perfect things. In boxing, you have to hone your skills and you have to be a pretty good boxer by the time you get to 20 years old, otherwise you're not going to be a good fighter. But in mixed martial arts, there's so many different avenues and ways to win a fight, and so many different ways you can be good at different skills, some of those backgrounds take years to get pretty good at. So it's where you start off; you have a huge background than boxers, this gives you time to go and do other things and go to school. Most of us fighters in MMA have wrestled before anyway.

Q: Do you feel the sport of MMA has become a lot more accepted nowadays?
Rashad Evans: It's getting there, to the point where it's not seen as violence. There are some pretty devastating knock outs that occur in some of the fights, but for the most part, the fans have learned a lot about mixed martial arts. They can understand and appreciate more technique. What I think is going to happen is

that the fans are going to be more educated about the fight. It'll get to a point when a fight hits the ground people aren't booing, that's what happens now some times.

The crowd wants to see someone getting knocked out or somebody bleeding. The fans still need to get to the point to appreciate the technique. If you watch a fight in Japan, you'll see the fans are so quiet, they appreciate all the little technique along the way. But the fights in the U.S and other places, fans are booing if you're not throwing a punch or knocking some one out in a minute or two. There's still a long way to go before the fans really appreciate all the little things and factors that the sport has to offer.

Q: Your first exposure to the UFC was when you watched the earlier shows with your friend. Is it true you made a decision that one day you'd love to fight in the UFC?
Rashad Evans: Yes. Me and my friend used to watch the UFC when we were babysitting his kids. In school, we always had this question; "Who would win against if a boxer such as Mike Tyson fought Bruce Lee." We were always wondering and trying to figure out which would be the best style that would beat everybody. When we saw the UFC for the first time, I was like, "Yo, man! I'm gonna one day do that, man." At the time we were taking a martial arts style called Tang So Do, and we were like mimicking all the time.

Q: What did you think of Royce Gracie when you witnessed him in the early UFCs?
Rashad Evans: I love Royce Gracie. Royce Gracie to me, is a huge inspiration, he's the man! Royce Gracie is the man! He gave me so much hope because I was never the biggest guy, my brother was always bigger and everybody was bigger than me. I was always the little guy and I always hung out with my brother's friend, who was a lot bigger than me. But when I'd seen Royce grappling with guys twice his size and this and the

other, it gave me hope. I realised it wasn't about being a bigger guy, but more about technique and what you know. So I didn't worry about being a little guy anymore; Royce is a big inspiration to me. He's excellent; he's the father of the sport.

Q: You love fighting. Is it true you once said to yourself "Why fight on the street when you can get paid for it?" When did you make a decision to pursue your MMA dream?

Rashad Evans: It was pretty much about street fighting which changed my perception of fighting on the street. One day on the street, when I was in college I was drunk and acting like a fool, like fools do when they are drunk. One time, I was not trying to fight, the fight actually came to me and I was actually trying to make peace with the person, and the guy sucker punched me, knocked me out cold. My head hit the concrete and I was knocked out cold, man. I was laid up for a couple of months and I couldn't even move my neck, totally messed up. That's when I thought to myself the fighting on the street is not worth it man. Then from that point on, I realised I wasn't invincible and I could really get hurt or do that to somebody else and even kill them. So l thought to myself, "It's not worth it!"

Q: You participated in TUF series 2, can you tell me of your experiences on this reality show?

Rashad Evans: I sent in a video tape and I got a call back and went and did the trials. They liked what they'd seen so it went from there. It was weird man, it was like fake reality imposed on you; you have cameras on you and all these different circumstances happening, you are kind of like a guinea pig. It's weird, because your whole reality is totally misconstrued just because you're in a house in a reality show. Once you get adjusted to the cameras, everything else is cool after that. But just being in a situation having to eat with people and then fighting them, this was very tough for me to deal with. I'm the kind of a person that I'm a friend for life, and I don't like to fight my friends. This was really hard for me to deal with. After I got over that it was business as usual.

Q: What was it like to finally step into the octagon?
Rashad Evans: It was a dream come true, a big dream come true. It was just unreal, I couldn't believe this is happening and I'm the one that people are watching on the TV. It was just like, "Wow", and truly amazing. I wanted to go home and watch the video. Then I was going through the motions of the whole thing and really had the chance to analyse everything, and I was like, "Damn, that's really me on there!" It was just a surreal moment.

Q: I understand your mom is actually a big Bruce Lee fan?
Rashad Evans: Yeah, my mom's a huge Bruce Lee fan! She always watched Bruce Lee films growing up and I was watching them too. She now tells me, "Rashad you gotta get your kicks right, like Bruce Lee." She's like the coach, Cus D'Amato. I'm like "OK! OK!" Sometimes her predictions are right, man. My mom's a big fan, and now she knows the moves and the sport. She would say "Rashad you gotta work on passing the guard like Joe Rogan said." I'm thinking "Damn, Joe Rogan's getting me in to trouble!"

Q: What are your own opinions on Bruce Lee?
Rashad Evans: I think Bruce Lee is a great inspiration and a great fighter and was ahead of his time. Now people are starting to realise what his message was. Was it not for mixed martial arts, people would just say, "Bruce Lee said this or whatnot." I think they would have appreciation for him, but not like now. Now they understand just how truly great he was, because he was there from the beginning experimenting with the MMA. He didn't believe one single style was the best; he was mixing all different styles to make a complete fighting style. He was saying it back then and people thought, "This dude's crazy!" He was

125

preaching it in his days and now people can see mixed martial arts, they can see that you need to have all these elements to become a great fighter ,and flow quickly into all of them.

Q: At UFC 73 you fought Tito Ortiz to a draw can you shed some light on this fight?
Rashad Evans: I really got caught up in all the trash-talking before the fight. I got out there but I didn't go out and grab the 'moment' as they say, but the moment took a hold of me. So that was the big problem. Instead of going out grabbing the moment, the moment got hold of me. Then before I knew it, I realise I'm in here about to fight Tito Ortiz, who I had watched fighting as I was growing up. I'm like, I'm about to fight this dude. So I was kind of a little gun shy in the beginning of the fight, but then I opened up a little bit but it was too late. Tito is good for the sport because whether you like him or you hate him, you want to see him, you want to see him fight.

Q: In UFC 84, you fought and beat Michael Bisping breaking his undefeated record as a pro. Do you have any comments on this fight?
Rashad Evans: I got this fight on a short notice, but Michael Bisping was coming in from a very controversial win. I had my mind set on fighting Tito Ortiz again, but that didn't happen. I went into the fight thinking, "I'll just go in there and get the fight over with." Michael Bisping came out and he was ready to go, he was charged up and he was a tough fighter than I actually anticipated. This is one of the fights where you go into a fight and you don't have any sick days, if you wake up in the morning of your fight and you feel like crap it's too bad, because you have to go in there and fight any way. That's what I was going through. Not taking away anything from Michael Bisping, because it would have been a tough fight anyway. I really wasn't feeling 100%, it was one of those days. But luckily I prevailed and pulled off the fight and a win.

Q: You have a clean record in the UFC as you are still undefeated. Do you feel any pressure at all?

Rashad Evans: I try not to think about my record too much, because that's when you fight from a mindset where you can't preserve something. When you have something to lose, the person who has nothing to lose usually ends up putting you in a situation where you feel you may lose what you are trying to hold on to. What I recently started to do is to have a mindset where I'm thinking, "You know what? I don't care anymore, I don't care about my record or anything like that, because the only thing that is important to me when I step into the cage is the fight right there, anything else doesn't matter to me." Once you know how to win, it's kind of a flow you always follow, so you know what you need to do to win the fight.

You think, "If I do this, or that, I can win the fight...", but that doesn't automatically happen. I need to take a little bit more chances, not being afraid of taking the chances because you're not afraid to lose. Confidence is the most important factor. You have to find the medium where you're not afraid, you're not afraid to lose and you're not afraid to go out there.

Everybody has, I don't care who they are, they have one thing in common; once they step into the octagon they're thinking, "Oh shit, this is going to be the day when I have to wake up in the locker room and have somebody tell me what happened, because I just got knocked out." Everybody has that feeling, but you have to go inside your mind and pass that, and say to yourself, "You know what? I don't give a damn. Today is the day because as long as I'm in there, this guys going to wish he's never ever has to fight me again, even if he sees my name on a piece of paper he's going to get the chill, he's not going to have anything to do with me after the fight!" It's hard to get that through your mindset.

Q: Do you feel MMA is a good outlet for African-Americans who traditionally get involved in boxing?

Rashad Evans: There will be more people getting involved, but it's a sport where the economics can make a difference. Because, in order to get good, to a level where you should be at, it's not something you can pick up on the street and do without too much instruction and get better yourself. You need proper instruction, you have to take Jiu-Jitsu classes, Muay Thai, boxing etc, and you have to pay for it. Sometimes you're in a situation where you are not able to do this. I think if there are any programmes which help out kids, who are athletes or any kids who are financially struggling then that would be great. When I have a gym, I'm hoping I can help kids and put them on a kind of like a scholarship programmes, which will to help kids to get into the sport.

Q: What was your family's reaction when you started fighting in the cage?
Rashad Evans: My mom was kind of surprised, she didn't really know actually how big it [UFC] was but people came to her and would talk to her about it. Then she really started to get more into it. But before she was just like, "Oh yes, you are going to fight". I was really a rough kid growing up and always trying to fight somebody and getting into mischievousness. She knew that's what I was good at. She wasn't really too surprised after I got into the TUF show. Now she's an expert at it, and she calls me and tells me what I need to work on in my training. Now she's a professional, like she's some great boxing coach like Cus D'Amato telling me what I need to do and work on, it's kind of funny.

Q: You said you wouldn't fight a friend in the octagon. Why is that?
Rashad Evans: It's true. I love my friends, man. When I have a friend, he's a friend for life and I'd do anything for my friends. When you train with somebody you kind of give a piece of yourself, because you want your training partner to be good too.

You want to be able to give something back to him, so when you exchange that, all the blood and tears that come along with training, it's hard to go in the octagon and fight somebody who is your friend and your training partner.

To fight somebody, you have to treat them like your enemy, in a way; you have to dislike a man to a point. Even though you don't dislike the person personally, you have to hate a man a little bit inside, even if it's just for that fight. For me, this is what I do.

Q: What did you think of facing Chuck Liddell in the octagon and were you surprised of knocking him out like you did?

Rashad Evans: I got a big opportunity to fight someone like Chuck Liddell, not only him but I want to fight the best. Sometime you kind of confuse yourself on which ones are your favourites to fight. Sometimes, I'm thinking Chuck Liddell is just another fighter like myself, then you think, "It's Chuck Liddell, the legend! Oh man! He's the icon and the one guy who puts his heavy fist on some body's chin!" - then you kind of focus on the fight.

When I went out there, I made myself comfortable, not getting caught up thinking too much about my opponent, like it's a big fight with a legend similar to how I felt against Tito Ortiz. It wasn't a fight where I felt comfortable right away and wasted a whole lot, and this ended up costing me. But this time I took the moment at the same time not getting myself caught up with it. So I went out there and made myself feel comfortable and it was just a matter of performing my game plan.

I knew I was going to win but I was just surprised on how it ended because of the very dramatic end. I trained really hard for this fight which showed. The one important shot knocking him out you could see how quite everybody was, once I knocked him out. I mean, you could have heard a pin drop in the arena once I performed the knock out and everybody saw Chuck on the floor. Everybody was like, "Aww!", you could hear a huge silence around the arena.

Q: What is your ultimate goal in the UFC. Is it winning the UFC belt?
Rashad Evans: Well I definitely want to win the belt and that's something I'm going to achieve, but more than anything I want to be a UFC great. I want something the guys in the future can look back at, and looking at the knock downs and think, "He was 'the man'." I want to make my mark.

As far as what it will feel like to be a champion, I think it'll be like when I became a junior college champion when I won the wrestling championship. After I won, there was a second of a pause... the excitement and everything was so short time, the moment of jubilation and excitement just came to the peak, and then it was gone. It was like "OK, I won it", and I was ready to move on. Not ready to move on from the sport but it was a feeling parallel to, "Now I've achieved the goal". I think it will be the same thing when I get the UFC belt.

You focus on getting the thing and then you finally get it. Even when you are the champion, the thing is in order to keep the belt you have to fight another champion, you have to stay hungry and fight like you're trying to get the championship. Then, if you can't stay hungry, you have to graduate from being hungry and be greedy. You have to say, "I used to be hungry, but now I'm greedy." You have to have that kind of a mindset. The way to keep that mindset is you have to fight everybody like a dog, it's like he's got something and you're trying to take it from him.

Q: What do you think of people criticising fighters and how do you take criticism?
Rashad Evans: I probably take more criticism than anybody, especially being undefeated. But it comes with the territory. I

used to get upset about it. But one thing my mom always said is, "You can't make someone like you". I go out there and give it my best, my best fights in me are definitely still ahead of me. Criticism is just criticism. People who criticise are people who don't do, anybody that does do, they criticise that person. It's a different game when you get in the octagon.

You're an entertainer and you put yourself out there, so you have to be able to take criticism because people are paying to see you. I accept criticism, but I know the difference. I don't let criticism take over control my head, I don't like doing that. People that always impose certain things on you, for instance, if I feel bad about myself I'm going to say, "You suck", that you're not good and what you can't do, because I believe that I can do it if I were you. People are going to impose weaknesses on you, so sometimes when someone criticises you, most of the times they don't even believe in themselves.

Q: Who is your favourite UFC fighter?
Rashad Evans: My favourite fighter has to be Randy Couture, because he's a great guy. I've trained with him and he's always been a straight up dude and beside that, he's a great fighter. He's one of my all time favourites. Also my good friend Georges St Pierre, because he brings it on each fight, sometimes very fearless and I admire that.

Q: You were a hospital security guard - a job you enjoyed - before becoming a UFC fighter. What does it feel like now you are making a living in the fastest growing sport in the world?
Rashad Evans: It's a whirl-wind! Sometimes I sit back and think, "Is this really my life now, is this really happening to me? Am I going to wake up one day and I don't have to put on my security uniform, is this really happening to me?" Sometimes it feels like that, because you have people coming up to you who are fans who you wouldn't have thought would be coming over

to talking to you. I met a lady in the church who is 60 years old coming over to me talking to me about fighting, and I couldn't believe it! I couldn't even believe she was even watching it. She was a big fan. It's amazing, my job working as a security guard was probably one of the best jobs I ever had, but this is far by 10 times better.

Q: How many more years will you be fighting professionally?
Rashad Evans: God willing, I don't know. In this game you are always one fight away from your last fight. Who knows how long I've got. I'm on God's time, he gave me the gift to fight and he's put it in my heart to be the fighter I am, and the fighter I'm going to be. And once that's over, when I'm done and I walk out of the door I'll find something else what God has in line for me. Who knows what this is going to be. I definitely would like to give something back to the sport, open up a gym. The reason I don't have one right now is I can't be the coach I would like to be, because I'm trying to learn a lot myself, and concentrating on the fighting and I won't be able to give back to me students.

TIM SYLVIA
'THE MAINE-IAC'

Timothy Dean Sylvia is a former UFC heavyweight champion who was influenced by the late Bruce Lee. Sylvia is one of those UFC fighters who went through a tough childhood, his parents were alcoholics and he suffered a great deal of abuse as he was growing up. However, things began to look up for him as he started wrestling in high school and took up karate.

Before entering the biggest MMA organisation - the UFC - Sylvia took part in various smaller events such as 'Extreme Challenge' and 'Superbrawl.' A natural striker, Tim won his first ever fight in mere 17 seconds, as he bashed his opponent unconscious with open hand strikes.

Being a big UFC fan right from the beginning, Sylvia's ultimate dream was realised when he was invited to fight in UFC 39 and he made the very most of his opportunity, as he hammered Wesley 'Cabbage' Correira in two one-sided rounds. In February 2003 he won the UFC heavyweight title by beating Ricco Rodriquez, only to lose it to Frank Mir in UFC 48, suffering a terrible broken arm at the hands of the Las Vegan. He regained the title in 2006, beating Andre Arlovski, before finally losing the crown to Randy Couture, in 2007.

Q: Tim, you endured a horrendous abuse from your parents who were both alcoholics, can you talk me through just how hard it was for you growing up?

Tim Sylvia: I think everyone knows my parents were alcoholics when I was growing up and my mother was very abusive, both mentally and physically. She decided that mentally would work better than physically. That's what I had to deal with my whole life, and even still today. Sometimes she would call and say, "You're a piece of shit you're not good enough." And if I lost a fight she would call and she'd laugh and say, "ha ha ha you lost, you suck," and so forth.

Q: You joined a karate school as a young kid and also enjoyed playing basketball, did you want to pursue a career in sports?

Tim Sylvia: No, not really, I was just doing it because it was fun. I liked martial arts and I was a big Bruce Lee fan obviously, he was definitely my hero.

Q: A lot of UFC fighters have been influenced by Bruce Lee, how would he fare in MMA?

Tim Sylvia: I felt he was 'the man' growing up, he was the badass fighter that we used to watch his movies and stuff like that, that's what worked for me and that's why I was doing karate. I wanted to be like Bruce Lee. Bruce Lee is an athlete and a mixed martial artist therefore he'd obviously learn to train jiu-jitsu and wrestling.

If he just had the mentality that his striking is the best and went out there and fought a MMA fighter he'd get taken down and ground and pounded. But Bruce Lee being the martial artist he is, he knows the way of mixed martial arts, I believe he would train properly for it and do very well.

Q: Your first No Holds Barred fight lasted a mere 17 seconds. But I hear you paid 50 dollars entry fee to compete?

Tim Sylvia: Yes I did, It was the 'Rhode Island Vale Tudo'. I was scared as hell, very scared, and he was the first fighter I fought. I was bouncing on the town and playing semi-pro football at the time, and I'd been in a few street fights but when you grapple a couple of times a week, you're learning - I wrestled in high school before that - so I was boxing and grappling couple of times a week to prepare for the fight.

Q: You became a UFC fan right from the beginning, when did you see the UFC for the first time?
Tim Sylvia: Yes I did. I saw the first UFC when I was in high school, I think. I had buddies who said to me, "You have to go to blockbuster movie store and see this, 'The Ultimate Fighting." They said there was this little Brazilian guy, Royce something - who, of course, was Royce Gracie - was beating everybody from the karate guys and other fighters, and he fights on the ground. It took me about two weeks to get the tape because everybody had heard about it and they were renting it. So when I saw it I was like, "Oh my goodness I love it!"

Q: When the UFC came to Atlantic City did you really drive for 11 hours with your buddies to watch the show?
Tim Sylvia: The guys that I trained with all had heard of the UFC and we were fans for previous years, six or seven years. The drive to Atlantic City was 11 hour drive and there were four of us, and we rented a mini van and drove down there. When we got there we started walking around and went the other way round and saw some people including [Ken] Shamrock, Tito [Ortiz] and the Miletch crew, it was pretty cool.

So before the fights we went down the lobby to see if we could catch any fighters going in, and get some pictures and autographs. As I'm walking with my buddies a security guard says, "Oh, it's you why don't you come on in." Because of my size and with my friends I'm assuming they thought I was Gan McGee, who was fighting that night with Josh Barnet. So we all walked in and there's Kevin Randleman warming up who was going to fight Randy Couture, and all the other fighters were all hanging out there. This was UFC 28, where Jens Pulver knocked out John Lewis.

Q: How did you get involved in the UFC?
Tim Sylvia: I was fighting a little bit and I met Pat Miletich that night, and we just started talking about fighting. He was really outgoing, I told him I had hard time finding fights as I was 6 ft 8, 240 pounds, and the fights I had scheduled did not often materialise, because when my opponents saw me they were like, "I ain't fighting him", and they'd leave. Pat said "Why don't you come to Iowa and train, come down for a couple weeks and if you like it then train with us." I took him up on the offer.

Q: What did it feel like when you entered the cage for the first time?
Tim Sylvia: It was crazy, I was fighting [Wesley] Cabbage Correira and he was someone I wanted to fight. I was going to fight him in a previous event called 'Superbrawl', but he had faked an injury so he could fight in the UFC. It was just awesome, the electricity and the crowd, me being in the UFC, how big the cage was, it was pretty nerve racking.

Q: You fought Randy Couture who is, no doubt, one of the greatest UFC fighters ever. What do you remember from your battle against him?
Tim Sylvia: It was a hard fight. I went into the fight injured and him being a good friend of ours, I probably just didn't take it like it was going to be a 'fight'. I thought, 'Oh, it's just Randy' - like I was just going for a sparring session. When he hit me with that overhand right and knocked me out for the first 20 minutes - I didn't know where I was.

Then the 5th round came and Pat is yelling to me,

"You're gonna knock him out, you're behind, you're behind on points", and I'm like, "I'm going to knock him out in the second round ", my corner is telling me "No this is the 5th round," and I'm like "Oh, OK". Randy is a great friend of mine.

Q: Would you say you are a natural fighter or did you have to learn a lot to prepare for MMA fights?
Tim Sylvia: I'm a natural fighter, definitely; I was born fighting, I've been fighting for my life since I've been born. But you have to train in MMA, I had to train in jiu-jitsu, Muay Thai and the boxing; I mean, I trained my ass off! Everything comes to me because of hard work.

Q: Tell me about the most disturbing sports injuries that you sustained when you fought Frank Mir.
Tim Sylvia: Well, I went into that fight with a little a bit of anger because Frank was talking some shit. So I went into the fight angry and not really composed. I was like, "I'm just going to kill this guy." So I made a mistake. I took him down and I thought I'd be on the ground and I'm just going to ground and pound him. He went for the armbar and my elbow popped out and I broke my arm. And I'm like, "He's just broke my arm I'm just going to kill him."

After the injury, I never wanted to stop fighting, I just wanted to get better and fight Frank Mir again. Going into the Arlovski fight I was still a little timid, when he put a toe hold on me I felt my ankle pop a few times and I reached out and tapped out. I think if my arm hadn't been broken in the fight with Mir I might not have tapped prematurely and the fight might have ended differently. But maybe its good I did tap, because I'd rather have a broken arm than a broken leg or ankle. Because at least I can walk around and get around just fine, but with a broken ankle it's not good.

Q: What MMA shows did you compete in before fighting in

the UFC?

Tin Sylvia: I fought in 'Superbrawl' and 'Extreme Challenge' events. UFC is the big show and most fighter's goal is to be in the UFC eventually, that's where everyone strives to fight, and most fighters eventually want to take this avenue -it's the big show, it's the Super Bowl of mixed martial arts.

Q: You beat Andre Arlovski twice to regain the heavyweight belt. How do you rate him as a fighter?
Tin Sylvia: I'm bigger and stronger and a better striker than he is. The second fight I had against him, I kind of mentally got to him and I knocked him out, that's really easy to get to someone mentally. When we had another fight I said, "I'm going to knock him out again, he's got a weak chin and I'm going to knock him out again" - and that he's easy to knock out.

So I made him real timid, so when I hit him in the 3rd fight, I rocked him and gave him wobbly legs and he didn't want to engage anymore. He played it safe and wanted to stop the fight. Sometimes you can do this to fighters and sometimes you can't, but he's one of those fighters that I can get into his head very easily.

Q: Before you are fighting somebody do you check out your opponent by researching him?
Tim Sylvia: I watch some of his fights along with my trainers and establish a game plan and start training for that fight. We decide what we are going to do and how I'm going to oppose myself on my opponent.

Q: What has been your hardest fight?
Tim Sylvia: My hardest fight was probably with Randy Couture. I just got my ass kicked, I wish I wasn't that stubborn going into the fight injured, I think it would have been a different fight. Randy was a great guy that day, he had a great game plan and he kicked my ass for five rounds. I think if it

happens again, it'll be a different fight, I'm not saying I'm going to kick his ass but if it happens it'll be different.

Q: Can you compare the early UFC's in the No Holds Barred era to the sanctioned sport which we enjoy today?
Tim Sylvia: It's just a little more safer now for the fighters and the sanctioning makes it a sport now. Back then it was basically the Gracie's trying to prove that jiu-jitsu was the way of life and they could beat anybody. There weren't a lot of punches thrown back then because Gracie would take the opponent down and get in the full guard and submit his opponent. So there really wasn't a concern about the guys getting hurt and there were no gloves.

It's a sport now which has evolved, fighters have become good strikers and wrestlers and you see a lot more punches thrown now. Something had to be done because fighters were getting cut up on the knuckles, so the sanctioning bodies came in and made rounds and weight classes and this just made it better for the sport and make more money - and grow to where it's an actual sport now.

Q: Do you feel MMA fighters are real athletes?
Tim Sylvia: There's no question in my mind everybody in the UFC is an athlete, we are the hardest-training athletes in the world. Because it's not just like boxing where all you worry about is your hands and your roadwork. In boxing, you don't train your elbows knees, kicks, grappling and wrestling like we do. There's so much areas of training in our game that there's not enough hours in the week to get all the areas covered. It's difficult to because there is so many elements you have to cover in MMA.

Q: Were you ever influenced by any pro boxers? Boxers have been respected and widely thought to be the toughest men on the planet?

Tim Sylvia: I grew up watching Sugar Ray [Leonard], Marvin Hagler, [Mike] Tyson, but I wasn't really a big boxing fan until I started fighting in MMA.Then I started watching more boxing and I enjoyed that small part that had to do with our sport.

That's no longer true regarding boxers being the toughest guys on the planet, a boxer would never survive in the cage with us, or a ring, as long as it's MMA rules. I'm not saying everybody can compete, but I believe that I can beat any heavyweight boxer out there at his own game. I believe I can outbox any heavyweight boxer out there. I truly believe that my hands are that good. If they came into MMA then they wouldn't stand a chance.

Q: Was winning the UFC heavyweight belt your proudest moment in your career?
Tim Sylvia: The first time I won the belt it was cool, it just kind of happened; it wasn't a lot of hard work, I worked hard coming through the ranks but I fought one fight in the UFC and then they asked me if I wanted to fight for the UFC title. So it happened and I won. I was the heavyweight champ. Then having the belt and losing it and working my way back up to the rank, two loses in a row and Arlovski already beat me; going in there, getting knocked out and coming back and knocking him out, this really meant a lot to me the second time. It meant more to me the second time.

Q: What is your philosophy about fighting and life in general?
Tim Sylvia: You definitely have to surround yourself with good people, good trainers and training camps - someone you can trust who will be there for you. I have been with the Miletech camp for 10 years now and they are with me when I'm on the top or bottom. All the same guys are with me there like my family now.

Definitely you have to train hard, condition is important

so you have to bust your ass in the gym to make sure you're in peak performance. Conditioning is the only area you can control, you can't control submissions etc, but you can control your conditioning, so in the Miletich camp we make sure we bust our ass to make sure we are in great shape.

Q: Do you train with separate coaches who specialise in certain areas?
Tim Sylvia: We have everybody in the Milletch camp, we have got great wrestlers, great strikers, jiu-jitsu guys and boxers and so forth. I'm very fortunate in that I have some of the greatest heavyweights in the world in my gym. I bring in jiu-jitsu and boxing coaches to work with.

Q: You say you want to fight the best, how important is this to you?
Tim Sylvia: I'm a fighter first. I want to fight the best and prove myself I'm one of the best out there; therefore, I need to keep fighting the other best to prove that.

Q: Do you take part in any mental preparations before a fight?
Tim Sylvia: There's a lot, especially weeks before the fight, sitting in the corner thinking what I'm going to do to the guy. Warming up, shadowboxing, a lot of visualisation etc, that's about it, nothing too serious.

Q: Do you feel the UFC and MMA will grow beyond our expectations in the near future?
Tim Sylvia: We're taking over the world! MMA is going to take over the world. If you look at all these celebrities and pro athletes, such as football players, soccer players they're all coming to watch us. They know we are the next generation and the next big thing. These guys watch us and like us, it's cool when you get these people come watching a mixed martial arts event.

Q: What are your future plans?

Tim Sylvia: I have four or five years left fighting as long as I stay injury free. Just planning on being dedicated and working on my legacy and when I'm done fighting, I'll be doing hunting full time. I love to hunt and I've got a hunting company. It definitely relaxes me and takes me away from the fighting when I'm out in the woods - fighting doesn't even come to in my mind. I go out there and enjoy the great outdoors. I just enjoy been in the outdoors. Thanks to all the fans still following me, I'm not in the UFC anymore but with Affliction and Adrenaline MMA, thanks for all the support.

DAN SEVERN
'THE BEAST'

Dan 'The Beast' Severn is a UFC Hall of Famer who was an accomplished amateur and professional wrestler before making his UFC debut in 1994 at UFC 4 and was the first world class wrestler to enter the organisation.

Severn's memorable debut saw him plant the smaller Thai boxer, Anthony Macias, on his head with a series of devastating suplexes, before finishing both Macias and semi-final opponent, Marcus Bossett, with a pair of rough-and-ready rear naked chokes. After a classic 17-minute tournament final with Royce Gracie, Severn was famously triangle choked into submission by the crafty Brazilian. However, despite this loss, the American persisted with his new found career and has since racked up over 80 wins in MMA competition.

Still active, Severn's career spans three decades and over 100 fights, making him one of the most experienced MMA fighters in the world. He can also be found passing on the benefit of his experience to numerous students in his Coldwater, Michigan base; as he is the founder of a new mixed martial arts promotion called 'The Danger Zone.' Outside the Cage he's a gentleman, put him in the cage and he turns into a beast.

Q: Dan, you have an impressive wrestling background, tell me about it!

Dan Severn: I started in amateur wrestling back in 1969. In junior high school in the seventh grade, I was in the high school wrestling team and good enough to end up getting a full athletic scholarship to go to Arizona State University. I'm from Michigan, but I lived in Arizona for ten years between going to college and wrestling and also coaching at the university. Job opportunities brought me back to the state of Michigan. During my high school years I started doing freestyle and Greco Roman wrestling. By my freshman college I ended up doing sambo and judo. From then I just started competing in various types of events and going to National and State championships in amateur wrestling. I ended up doing my first main cup contest in the early 90s as of the '92 Olympics.

I started doing professional wrestling after being approached by several companies in the early 80s. I thought this was my chance to live the life style of a professional athlete. I used my real name and my amateur credentials .There was a gentleman there from Tennessee who asked me if my record was legit and I told him that it was. He said I ought to be in Japan competing in a thing called 'shoot-fight' or 'shoot-fighting', which I hadn't heard of before. So I gave him my business card and he gave one to me.

Three days later I got a phone call and one week later I had trials and a month after that I was in Tokyo getting ready to take part in my first shoot fighting match. Into the fight, I didn't know what I was doing but my Japanese opponent kicked me about four or five times really hard. I grabbed him, threw him all over the place and went crazy. The guy who brought me over said, "Dan Severn, you will become a superstar in Japan". Then in 1994 it was the beginning of my No Holds Barred mixed martial arts career in the Ultimate Fighting Championships and I've had a dual career ever since.

Frank Shamrock is one of the most dedicated Mixed Martial Arts athletes in the world

UFC Interim Heavyweight Champion Antonio Nogueira at a martial arts trade show

Anderson Silva, Leo Negao and Antonio Nogueira

UFC Poster Boy
Michael 'The Count'
Bisping

Former UFC Light-Heavyweight Champion Chuck Liddell is no doubt one of the biggest UFC stars on the planet

'Huntington Beach Bad Boy' Tito Ortiz, former UFC Champion and one of the most controversial characters in the sport

Former 'Pride' Middleweight Champion and UFC star Wanderlei Silva poses for the camera

UFC Middleweight Champion Anderson 'The Spider' Silva in action

UFC Hall of Fame member Randy Couture

Royce Gracie with cousin and training partner Rodrigo after a workout at the Long Beach Academy in Southern California

UFC Hall of Fame member Dan Severn ready to do battle.

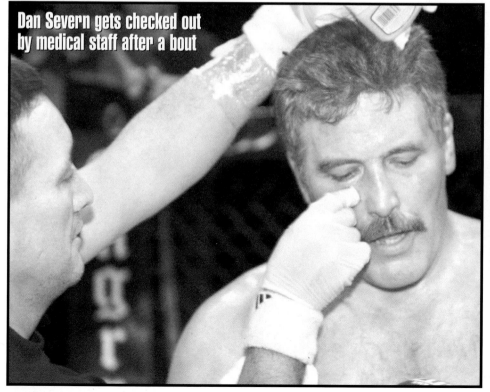

Dan Severn gets checked out by medical staff after a bout

UFC star Michael
Bisping enters the cage

Ken Shamrock
in action

Anderson 'The Spider' Silva lands a hard Thai-style kick on his opponent

'The Spider' dominates his opponent on the ground

Royce Gracie attacks Boxer Art Jimmerson in the first ever ground breaking UFC held in Denver, Colorado

Legendary Royce Gracie chokes out Ken Shamrock - UFC I

'Ground and Pound' Bisping style

Vitor Belfort warming up pre-fight

Vitor Belfort - the youngest UFC Heavyweight in history - working out with the focus pads before a fight

'Huntington Beach Bad Boy' Tito Ortiz, one of the most controversial characters in the sport

UFC Hall of Fame member Ken Shamrock will always be remembered as one of the pioneers of the sport of MMA

Below: Gracie Jiu Jitsu 'Hits Hollywood: Royce Gracie and brother Rorion - the creator of the UFC - on the set of 'Lethal Weapon' movie with actor Danny Glover

Tito Ortiz poses for a professional publicity photo shoot for his 'Punishment Athletics'

Q: You were the first world class Olympic style wrestler to enter the UFC, how did you get involved?

Dan Severn: I live in a rather rural community and still do, but it was so rural at the time that they didn't have the pay-per-view capabilities. So a friend of mine out of Detroit had watched the first couple of UFC's and he brought them to me and showed them to me. He said, "Hey you oughta think about doing this!" It was people getting stomped in the face, and I told him, "These aren't exactly skills I possess".

He said, "Look at this skinny little guy doing Jiu-Jitsu", of course he was referring to Royce Gracie. So here I am I'm watching the tapes and I said to him that it kind of looks like wrestling. And thought, if someone is close enough to kick or punch me I can either step out of the range or step in close them down where they can't really get much velocity in the strike. That's when I kind of thought I'd do OK in a competition like this.

So I sent in an application but no one ever called me back. I was told that the UFC were receiving between two and three hundred applications on a daily basis. So a few more calls were made to the match maker Art Davie. I happen to be going to Los Angeles on a professional wrestling card. So Art came down and watched me in my professional wrestling match and then conducted his personal interview with me. The first thing he said to me was, "You do realise what we do is real don't you"? And I said I knew, and he asked me what my professional wrestling record was, and I told him I didn't have one. So he asked what my amateur record was. And I said I didn't have one of those either. So he asked me what my skills were. I said I was an amateur wrestler for 26 years.

He said, "Well amateur wrestling has rules and regulations". And I told him that was not necessarily true. I asked him if he ever had been to a foreign soil with a foreign referee, you'd be surprised what you can do. He asked me what I meant by that, I said to him, "Let me reiterate my very first international experience ever at 17 years of age."

I was part of the U.S all star team and at 16 to 18 years old we went to the country of Turkey. We were supposed to be wrestling Turkish wrestlers who were between the ages of 15 and 18. My first opponent was a 35 year old military man, who was muscular, with his meanness and ugliness, and he's walking back and forth like a caged animal. And here I am a 17 year old slender built wrestler, I had all my hair back then in the early 1970s!

The match started and he grabbed back of my hair and head butted me splitting my eye brow open. Then he tears a lot of hair out and slings it on the ground, my hand is up on the side of his head and blood is stripping down my face. I look at the referee to see if the match is over thinking my opponent is going to be disqualified for non sportsmanship conduct. All the referee did was simply step in between us and kicked the hair on the ground out of the way - and he cautions me for passivity.

This happened to be in the first 15 seconds of the match. Matches at the time were 3 minutes 30 seconds long with a 1-minute break in between rounds. You didn't even stop for blood because it was normal - you got bloody noses all the time. They did not stop the matches; if you had a bloody nose or split lip you reached in you wiped it and kept going, there were no time outs for that kind of stuff.

So the guy split my head and now I'm mad and angry and I channel my anger through my technique. I go for a hard double leg takedown and we hit the ground. In wrestling you don't want to be on your back so he turns around. There's a technique called the cross face where you get the bridge of your arm across the soft tissue.

Now I had anger running through my body and I broke his nose, and his blood is pouring out of his nose all over my arm. I've got pain shooting up my arm because he's biting into my forearm trying to take a chunk of meat out of me. So at that point I decided to hurt him really bad. I reached up and grabbed my own arm and I was trying to jam it into his nose and skull, basically I was trying to kill him. Just because he inflicted injury to me, in return I was trying to inflict even more injury to him. Referee blows the whistle and pulls my arm off his nose and he penalises me for an illegal manoeuvre. I show him the teeth marks on my arm and he penalises the Turkish opponent for an illegal manoeuvre.

At the end of the first 3-minute round, the referee sends me back to my corner and sends my opponent back to his. We were both a bloody mess! His coach was so angry that a little weeny-looking American is ahead of him in points that he pulled out a stick thickness of a broom handle, and proceeded to beat his athlete. I've had people saying, "No you're kidding me!" - but I have lived that experience.

Q: Can you talk me through your epic battle with Royce Gracie, did he surprise you?
Dan Severn: I don't know if he surprised me. Before entering the UFC I only had two UFC video tapes to watch and he was in both of those. So I kind of knew what he was all about. The thing is, I'm not going to make any excuse, at the time I was told I was going to be in the upcoming UFC It was kind of a last minute fill in. I only trained for 5 days, an hour and a half each day and that was it. So I walked into, not only his world, but the world of No Holds Barred and held my own not knowing a single strike or a single submission, not even practising a single submission or strike.

I had a training camp with three professional wrestlers and we went inside the professional wrestling ring with an old pair of boxing gloves and the name of the game was, "Try to punch Dan and Dan doesn't like to be hit". So I was parrying the punches and getting into upper body clinches or take downs and slapping on an amateur wrestling move and turning it a little illegal. That was my training camp. So it was almost a joke in itself.

I didn't throw any strikes in my first two matches. I did after several minutes had passed in the match with Royce Gracie himself, then I had to think about it because I had fought for 26 years under rules and regulations. I was struggling more with my conscious than I ever had with an opponent against Royce Gracie. I don't mean to say that in a derogatory sense, but that is how it was. Had I simply cut loose, it might have been a different outcome of the match, but I'll live with my decision which was to do what I did at the time.

Q: After your experience in UFC 4 did you revaluate your training approach?
Dan Severn: I actually went back to train as I had time now. By contract, they could not get rid of me as long as I finished in the top two, so I was automatically invited back. I like to think that I was the monkey which hit the system because a lot of people don't realise the company was half owned by the Gracie family and half owned by Art Davie. So I really questioned if it was a real competition, I mean they were real fights but I think people may have been hand selected.

Q: Any behind the scenes UFC stories you'd like to share?
Dan Severn: The funny part was that one of the guys who traveled with me, Al Snow who was a professional wrestler. Al Snow was wearing the typical muscle t-shirt and I was wearing a suite and a tie. Whenever we were walking around everybody thought I was his manager and he was the fighter. Then at the day of the press conference where it was going to be announced who was going to fight who, Al Snow was sitting in the crowd while I was sitting up on stage with the other seven men.

Q: Do you feel Olympic wrestling is one of the hardest sports? Have many wrestlers competed in MMA?
Dan Severn: Yes they have because there's no true professional

outlet for them. If there was a real professional outlet for Olympic wrestlers then they would pursue that. But there isn't one. There's no real money that can be gained in amateur wrestling. Football players go play professional football, basketball players can turn professional, golfers and gymnastics can do the same. But real wrestlers, other than professional wrestling - which if you get into it - is basically entertainment and you're an actor and a stuntman basically.

There's a lot of amateur wrestlers that look down on professional wrestling. I think with the mixed martial arts it is a benefit to the wrestlers and the assets they bring into it teaches you a lot of body mechanics and body control. It doesn't teach you striking or submissions, but I have had a lot of Jiu-Jitsu practitioners and Muay Thai practitioners who come to learn wrestling from me. So, now they can incorporate it into their martial arts.

When you look at most Jiu-Jitsu practitioners, they're terrible at take downs. Any Jiu-Jitsu practitioner that is any good at takedowns somewhere along the way worked with a wrestler because the mechanics wrestling teaches you are good for takedowns. But Jiu-Jitsu is good once you hit the ground though.

Q: Lets talk about your controversial superfight against Ken Shamrock!
Dan Severn: He basically beat me on my first outing but at the same token there should never have been a first outing. I come from the world of amateur wrestling so if there's going to be a super fight basically it has to be between two people who've actually won things. At that point in time, Ken Shamrock hadn't won anything. The closest he had been was, I think, a runner up. To me, a runner up in wrestling never made it to super bouts and they never made it to championship bouts, they are still a runner up. Only the top people make it to championship bouts. I beat him the second time.

Q: Some MMA athletes are using steroids now, do you think Ken was on some kind of substance at the time he fought you?
Dan Severn: I don't think it's a lot of steroids they are using now but a lot of them are prone to human growth hormones because there are no tests for human growth hormone, but there are for steroids; so, more athletes are moving over to human growth hormone. I have to say Ken was on something, because he has faced Tito Ortiz at 205 pounds, Ken has been as high as 245 or 250 pounds range when he faced me. How do you put on that muscle mass in that short period of time?

I only know one way, and that's through chemistry. The thing about me is I'm a life-time chemical free and there's not too many heavy weights that can actually claim life-time chemical free status. If you only knew how little I trained in all of these years and still came away with the results I have... I'm a freak of nature.

Q: Which has been your toughest fight to date?
Dan Severn: The hardest fight would have been with another wrestler because the skills I bring in, and if he had the kind of wrestling skills to match then that would have neutralised each other's skills and bring into play then secondary skills. By secondary skills, I mean striking ability, whether it's your hands or feet to would determine the fight.

Q: You are an educated man and have a college degree, why did it take the public to realise UFC is not about two thugs fighting?
Dan Severn: I would disagree with the way you stated that. I think the general population loved it [the UFC]. I just think it was the politicians and athletic commissioners that had the misconceptions. Senators John McCain was one of the biggest detractors of the sport, yet he knew nothing about it. I was conducting two of my training camps held in Arizona at the North Phoenix Baptist Church which he is a member of. Right

in the basement of his own church, they have a youth programme called 'Rosy Cheeks'. They had five-year old kids who were doing open glove shots to each others face. That's why they came up with the name 'Rosy cheeks'. This was in his own church and he didn't even know about it.

Q: In your opinion how has the UFC evolved?

Dan Severn: UFC is just one company, it's the most recognised company but you've got EliteXC that is doing some great things , then you've got 'Showtime', HBO is getting to work with some promotion too. CBS just aired the Kimbo Slice against James Thompson fight. I'm happy with that because UFC needs competition. As more competition arises the athletes will be compensated better. When you look at what boxers are making one big super bout they're making millions of dollars. The very top UFC guys, by the time they get a piece of the pay-per-view, it's a little over than a million dollars for either one individual or a pair. I think it's going to grow and you are going to see more changes which will start to occur. There might even be more rules along the way. Still corporate America has not embraced it yet, there's a lot of growth yet to come and financial purses will grow as well.

Q: Is there any particular fighter you would liked to have fought who would it have been?

Dan Severn: It would have been Royce Gracie. Had I known just a little bit about the politics, I have nothing against Royce Gracie or his family, I'm not trying to attack anybody but had I known a little bit more what that company represented and how it was being run I would have done some different things in my match and it might have been a different outcome. Might have been, I can't guarantee that but I would have had a different mindset let's put it that way.

Q: What was the public's reaction when you made a

transition from MMA to WWE again?

Dan Severn: I was a professional wrestler first in 1992 before embarking on my MMA career. Then in 1994 the Ultimate Fighting Championships started out and later I ended up with working with WWF - now known as WWE - I had always been a professional wrestler first. A lot of people in the fight world think I was a sell out to the fight world when I went to professional wrestling, but the reality is I was a professional wrestler first. They shouldn't be mad at me but the only people who should be mad at me are the professional wrestlers because I sold out and became a cage fighter.

When I tell people now they think that's fine, now it's become a catch-22 kind of a thing for me; I didn't go to the WWF for the money, I went for the exposure. The UFC was a very small niche market in the beginning when it was known as No Holds Barred because you had Senator John McCain and other politicians and athletic commissioners trying to eliminate No Holds Barred fighting altogether. It had to change in order to survive. I am the only triple crowned champion from the No Holds Barred era that will be marked in the history books because No Holds Barred fighting doesn't exist anymore. This is a title I will hold forever.

Q: Who is your favourite UFC or MMA fighter?

Dan Severn: I couldn't even say, I just don't watch it enough to render an opinion, I very rarely watch it.

Q: What has been the proudest moment in your MMA career?

Dan Severn: I would say a couple of things; being the only triple crown champion in the UFC history in No Holds Barred era, that's one aspect. Then the Hall of Fame, which to me is a very political type of thing because we have new ownership. To me, it's like, who is voting in for these athletes? Who voted Randy Couture or Mark Coleman, who voted me in? Who is on the selection committee? Because I don't know if some people who are inducted into the Hall of Fame is because there were some political reasons behind that. I don't know. I mean, I look at it from a couple of different ways, but It's an honour to be recognised, but just because you have third ownership of the UFC is it Dana White and a few of the people in his office that decide who gets to go in the Hall Of Fame?

Q: You were one of the many UFC fighters to cross over to Japan and fight in Pride. What are your thoughts on fighting in Japan?
Dan Severn: Its different fighting in a ring opposed to a cage. I don't like the fact that if you get tangled up in the ropes in a ring because they stop you trying to pull you out in the centre and restart you, because that's kind of a tough thing to do because if you were in a bad position, you're going to go for a better position, that's human nature. That's the thing I didn't really like about it, I rather know if I'm in a cage I can use that cage to my advantage against my opponent. I'm one of the best guys using the cage as part of my tactics.

Q: Any advice for anyone wanting to get into MMA?
Dan Severn: I'd say train hard, do not give up your day job and hopefully your day job has health benefits.

Q: We hear some WWE wrestlers wanting to fight in the UFC, Kurt Angle has showed interest. How do you see them performing in the octagon?
Dan Severn: Kurt Angle has been talking about that for the last three or four years, but I don't think we'll see him jump in the Ultimate Fighting Championships. He might go into a smaller MMA company but I can't see him walking into the UFC. On the other hand Brock Lesnar is younger and would have more of a future. Other Professional wrestlers like Kurt Angle and Brock Lesnar, who were both amateur wrestlers and

were very good amateur wrestlers, could.

If you take an athlete who has a certain mind set with a work ethic would do just fine in other sport endeavors because the work ethic is strong, they know they have got to work hard and have this mental mindset. I think Brock would do just fine in his upcoming matches. He was little bit young to be put against Frank Mir, but at the same token had it been me training Brock Lesnar the match wouldn't have gone to the ground in the first place, in the first round. I would have taught him to keep hitting Frank out of his reach, bludgeoning him, bludgeoning him, and bludgeoning him.

I can't see Frank going to take Brock Lesnar down. Maybe stand for the first round and second round and then go on the ground finish him off. Brock is a very powerful individual and most wrestlers can win with takedowns and ground and pound. Mir is good enough in submissions and, early on, he can catch a leg or arm and he'll finish it.

Q: What are you involved in presently?
Dan Severn: I'm sitting here in my office inside of a 10,000ft training facility in Coldwater, Michigan. It's called 'Michigan Sports Camp Training Facility'. We teach amateur wrestling which still is my first teaching because I've been doing that for longer than anything else. We also teach professional wrestling and we have athletes going onto WWE and TNA and a lot of the independent circuits. Once a month we run pro shows inside of our training facility. We also teach mixed martial arts and I have several other instructors teaching boxing, kick boxing, Muay Thai, jiu-jitsu.

I've been working with law enforcements for over six years and developed defensive tactics. They've had several states come up to our facilities because of our effective methods which are very functional for what they need to do. I continue to do a lot of mixed martial arts seminars, speaking engagements, appearances, and last year I fought in 10 matches and three matches already this year. I still have a few more matches to do this year, but the reality is I turn 50 years old as of tomorrow. I'm not the young man I once was but I started my UFC career just before I was 37 years old.

My MMA company is called 'Danger Zone'. We run a show every couple of months. We've run 36 total shows so far and have had people like 'Rampage' Jackson who competed earlier in his career, also Forrest Griffin, Sean Sherk, Ric Clementi to name a few. I also helped Rashad Evan's amateur and pro career and helped him get his video out to 'The Ultimate Fighter' show. He's a high profile athlete in UFC now. I have a degree from Arizona State, a teacher's certificate and right now I'm probably teaching a few times each month, as my schedule permits.

I engage students and make them think for the first time in their lives, that's what the administration loves about what I do. So you might have a fighter with a ring name 'The Beast' but I'm probably the furthest thing from it. This ring name was given to me by Jim Brown, the legendary football player. He said, "You're like Dr Jekyll and Mr Hyde; you're the nicest guy in the world outside of the cage, you wear suits and ties which make you look like an insurance agent - and when you step inside the cage, you bring a whole different image!"

He couldn't believe how I was able to do that transition. I got kind of giddy there, Jim Brown who is one of the top 100 athletes ever and for that man to give me my ring name, that is another one of those honours. The world record was 7 title belts when I started. I had 18 title belts. I started MMA at the age of 37. I'll probably pick up at least one more before I retire. I will probably retire because in a year-and-a-half or two years because I have some other interests that I want to pursue. I don't want to do injustice, I feel like I've been doing some injustice to my MMA career which has lasted more than 10 years. Anyway, I've had some loses which I ended up with which should have never occurred. Because the lack of training and preparation I ended up going into the matches and losing them otherwise I could've done otherwise. I do MMA seminars and If people want to learn some good mechanics when it comes to mixed martial arts, then I'm the man.

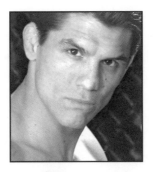

FRANK SHAMROCK

Frank Shamrock (born Frank Alisio Juarez III) was the first UFC fighter to hold the UFC middleweight championship title (which was later reclassified as the UFC light-heavyweight championship). He is considered a legend of the sport of mixed martial arts. The submission fighter started in mixed martial arts in 1994, fighting for the innovative Japanese promotion, Pancrase where he tasted early success against the likes of Bas Rutten and Vernon 'Tiger' White.

Frank later made his UFC debut in December 1997, where he defeated Kevin Jackson to be crowned UFC middleweight champion. After administering a vicious beat down to John Lober at UFC Brazil, Shamrock made the unprecedented step of retiring from the UFC as the five-time defending, undefeated champion.

Like his adopted brother, Ken Shamrock, Frank had a tough upbringing and was placed in foster homes before finding a path in life which would propel his name and fame around the globe. Frank is an exceptional combat sports athlete and physical specimen with a hard rigorous training regime which is equaled by very few. Today, he continues to fight and runs his gyms and MMA company from his base in San Jose.

Q: Let's talk about you childhood, you grew up in a rough environment where it was all about survival.
Frank Shamrock: I first left home when I was 12 years old, and that put me in the juvenile system. I went from one home to another home, about five different group houses. I ended up at the 'Shamrock Boys Home', that's where I met Ken Shamrock and Bob Shamrock. That's where my life changed from a street kid to a martial arts guy. It was really hard, growing up; I felt I was alone a lot because I never had my regular family. It was more about survival for me, I didn't really know any different. I came from a broken home with a lot of brothers and sisters and I always kind of felt I was really alone and always kind of looking for my family and reconnect to a community or something. So I remember being lonely and confused when I was growing up.

Q: When did you start training in the martial arts and what system did you take up?
Frank Shamrock: I started when I was 21 years old, and the first system I trained in was submission wrestling, which is 'Pancrase' based martial arts style.

Q: Did you ever take up wrestling or boxing prior to this as a kid?
Frank Shamrock: No, I was completely the opposite in that I never did any martial arts or any sports. I never really did any of these until I walked into the gym one day and started the whole wrestling thing. I started weight training when I was about 14, and I did that consistently for about 10 years.

Q: When did you first hear about and see the UFC?
Frank Shamrock: Actually I started training in submission wrestling before I ever saw the UFC. I watched my first UFC after about 4 or 5 months of training. I came from weird situation because I didn't want to keep going to community college but I wanted to live at home with my dad - my adopted

dad - who was an avid sports person. He suggested I go down and try wrestling, submission wrestling, the thing my brother was doing at the time. I walked into the gym and the martial arts not really knowing rules or anything. So it was a pretty much eye opener, my first experience.

Q: What did you think of someone like Royce Gracie, who was beating up bigger stronger guys?
Frank Shamrock: It was amazing, the whole art itself. I didn't really know much or studied UFC at the time, my study was submission wrestling and Pancrase which was from Japan - I understood the dynamics of submission. I thought the UFC was really crazy and barbaric at the time, I thought it was more of a street fight than actual martial arts. But I was always impressed with the submission ability and thought the submissions were kind of the key to winning fights.

Q: When did you first start training for the UFC?
Frank Shamrock: For me it was just an evolution of technique. I won the King of Pancrase championship and after that it was just like, "Where do you go next?" So the next big show was the UFC. I began training in mixed martial arts in 1997 and won the UFC title about six or seven months later. My first match was for the middleweight title, just after gloves became mandatory and just before weight classes. I remember the fight vividly. I fought Kevin Jackson for the middleweight title and I ended up beating him in 14 seconds. What I remember most about the match was the size of the cage which was very different than a ring and, inside the cage, the dynamics were very different. I had done big competitions in the Pancrase organisation and I had fought pretty big matches in front of large crowds before, so I didn't feel nervous in that way, but I felt nervous that I could get hurt and this worried me.

Q: What was it like fighting in Japan before and after your

UFC career?

Frank Shamrock: My most memorable fights were with Bas Rutten. He was a mad man! He was there to fight to the death and he had a different mentality than everybody else. I had the kind of a sportsman's mentality, whereas he had the kind of street fighter mentality. Different feeling made all the matches tough and really memorable.

Q: Can you talk to me about your UFC battles with Tito Ortiz?

Frank Shamrock: It was a huge turning point for me in my career. I beat everybody so fast and dominated the whole sport for a long time. He was the new generation of fighters, big strong guys who knew how to wrestle and it was a big test for me physically to go out and do battle with him. I took serious damage but I learned a lot about leverage, technique, conditioning and it was a big match for me.

Q: What is your 'on season' training conditioning regime?

Frank Shamrock: I do a lot of stuff for conditioning a month before I go out to the camp, so maybe two or three months out I do a lot of body weight muscular conditioning, like squats and push ups. Then, nearer to the fight, the conditioning becomes more explosive, so I do kettle bell training, plyometrics, jump training to condition muscles that are going to explode. My core is the key to all punching power and kicking power and wrestling conditioning as part of my muscular conditioning.

Then I train with weights, I love lifting weights, it's good for your bones and body. This I do a couple of times a week. Then 2 weeks before my fight I drop all my conditioning and relax and work techniques. Pad work, I separate it into two sections where I do a boxing work out and a kick boxing work out. On my boxing work out I always work 5-minute rounds and usually work myself up to five or six rounds; so 25, or 30 minutes of constant pad work.

For my kick boxing work out I lean towards more technique than anything because the technique will also aid in building up the conditioning and balance. I do this for five or six rounds as well and, probably one or two days, I kick really hard working on my power kicks, and those are all done on Thai pads. I used to do about four rounds of power kicks.

Grappling is something I do every day. I think the difference between the grappling style that I do is the positioning doesn't really matter as much in our style. Movement and fluidity of movement and transition and submissions are the most important things. So most of my grappling work outs consist of matt drills, partner drills or technical or wrestling where we just changing position quickly, looking for holds. I do this 30 or 40 minutes a day, then I do 50 to 60 percent working the technique where I'm just doing technical drilling.

Q: You're an advocate of weight training, conditioning and fitness, what weight training routine do you implement into your work outs to keep in top physical condition?

Frank Shamrock: I've got a real simple method; I always do three sets and three exercises for each large muscle group. For small muscle groups such as biceps and triceps, I work them once or twice a week and I do two sets and two exercises each part. For biceps I like the barbell curl and the preacher curl. For triceps my two favourites are seated triceps exercises. Shoulders are in between the small and medium muscle groups. I usually train them as a small muscle group "twos and twos".

I like the in-front of the face shoulder press, and side lateral dumbbell raises. For upper-back my favourite exercise are the seated row and anything pulling down like a seated pull down. In addition to these two exercises, my other two favourites are upward row with a barbell and one-arm pull up with a dumbbell. Lower back, abs and neck I tend to train every day. I do a set of 100 reps. I'll do a hundred crunches, the next day 100 leg raises and the next day 100 side bends. For lower back I do 100 hyperextensions or any other lower back exercise I can add in.

My legs are broken into two parts, the front and the back part. I train these every week. Actually, I do legs twice a week if you look at it. I do three exercises and three sets, with eight to ten reps. My favourite ones are 45 degrees leg press, the hack squat and the dumbbell lunge. The hamstrings and the calves, I do stiff dead lifts, also on the machine cable hamstring curls, and I work on the stability ball and do a hamstring curl on the ball. I don't really focus on calves as a specific part because I box every day, I spend about 30 or 40 minutes on the balls of my feet.

I think MMA fighters should be training with weights two or three days a week, preferably three days a week. The sessions should be an hour or hour and a half, high intensity. The goal should be, in my opinion, to strengthen and condition the body above and beyond, the muscle mass each muscle group being conditioned so the entire machine is strong.

Chest
Incline Bench Press - 3 sets 8-10 Reps
Dumbell Bench Press - 3 sets 8-10 Reps
Pull Overs - 3 sets 8-10 Reps
Biceps
Barbell Curl - 2 sets 8-10 Reps
Preacher Curl - 2 sets 8-10 Reps
Triceps
Triceps Dips - 2 sets 8-18 Reps
Triceps Dips 2 - 2 sets 8-18 Reps
Shoulders
In-front Shoulder Press - 2 Sets 8-10 Reps
Side Lateral Raises - 2 Sets 8-10 Reps
Upper Back
Seated Row - 3 Sets 8-10 Reps

Seated Pull down - 3 Sets 8-10 Reps
Legs (Front)
45 Degrees Leg Press - 3 Sets 8-10 Reps
Hack Squat - 3 Sets 8-10 Reps
Dumbell Lunge - 3 sets 8-10 Reps
Legs (Hamstrings)
Stiff Dead Lifts (Hamstring) - 3 Sets 8-10 Reps
Machine Cable Hamstring Curls - 3 sets 8-10 Reps

Q: How important is nutrition to you as a Professional athlete?
Frank Shamrock: First of all, food and nutrition is your fuel which runs your machine; for me, it's all about eating small meals, five or six small meals a day. Each meal, I try to consume about 20% protein, 20% carbohydrates. I always like to eat green, orange vegetables. I also add a protein drink after training. I also drink Electrolex in between my training and I drink lots of water.

Q: You coach a lot of fighters now, what are your coaching principles?
Frank Shamrock: I think the biggest thing that I teach is, physically and mentally, you can do whatever you want, and you can do anything as long as you prepare yourself for it. Conditioning, technique, whatever you want to accomplish. I'm a believer in meditation, focusing and creating the technique or the game plan you want to create, and the secret is of course hard work. My biggest success has always been being in the gym and training hard, and I teach my guys if you train hard and you focus and have a good plan then you can succeed.

Q: You are close with former UFC heavyweight Champion Maurice Smith, who was one of the first strikers to be crowned UFC champion. Did you make deal with regards to exchanging methods?

Frank Shamrock: I made a deal years ago where he would train me in striking and I would train him in grappling. So we've been doing that for about 12 years now. He's one of the best boxing and kickboxing striking coach you can get because he really understands the game. He's also always being a student learning new techniques and upgrades his methods. When you're always studying and always getting better, you're always getting more efficient and effective and he's one of those students of the arts that keeps me on my toes competing with you at anything which makes you stay on edge and focused.

Q: UFC has drifted into the mainstream now, how do you think a professional boxer would do in MMA?
Frank Shamrock: I think there's no doubt that punching people in the head causes the most deaths. There's no doubt about that. The problem is, when you mix the kicking, and the grappling, throwing and the submission holds, then all these have strength of value. So a straight boxer is never going to be as powerful as an all round MMA fighter. I definitely think boxers are not the best fighters in the world, but they are definitely the best punchers in the world. Punching is just one part of the game.

Every athlete would be good at mixed martial arts if they trained at it, because boxing is a very fine art which takes a long time to get good at, a lot of repetitions and training is required. MMA or even grappling is much more organic and natural styles, your body knows how to move and wrestle. It's very foreign to punch stuff, you have to train your body to do it; anybody with that kind of dedication and training would be good at MMA. Any boxer would be good at MMA if they trained MMA, if they didn't then they'd fall prey to technique just as someone who didn't know how to punch would fall prey to punching.

Q: MMA and UFC has broken into the mainstream, how do

you feel about this?
Frank Shamrock: It feels great! Being one of the leaders of the sport I knew the sport from the beginning will be as popular as it is today. It's an amazing art form, and when you get the right combination of social environment, like now, the sporting organisations right now, it realises its true potential. It's fantastic to be in the game right now.

Q: Did you coach BJ Penn at one time?
Frank Shamrock: Actually, he was a young guy who trained with me at the Shamrock camp at one point. I was impressed with his natural ability, amazing flexibility and his amazing balance. I think when he's focused and in shape he could beat everybody in the world.

Q: How has UFC evolved since you exited?
Frank Shamrock: The sport in the marketing aspects has definitely evolved, the techniques have evolved, but only slightly. The marketing, selling of the sport and promotion side of things have really evolved. The technical side has done so too but a lot slower than I would have wanted it to. Because truthfully, a lot of the information was still available seven or eight years ago, just now the athletes are getting masters in the way they look at us. Before it was martial artists mixing styles to get better, that's the game, now these people are truly training in all styles all the time. Much like Bruce Lee did with Jeet Kune Do, most people are just throwing away the stuff that doesn't work at all and not really worrying about it, just training the core techniques of MMA.

Q: Do you believe you were influenced by the late great Bruce Lee?
Frank Shamrock: When I was a kid he's the guy who really sparked my interest in martial arts. It was like being in school, there was always some lesson to be learned or some story from

his films. That was the first feed of martial arts I latched onto. When I got older, in my late teens, I started reading about him and his philosophies. He was the first person who was, in my opinion, looking at this very old art form in a very spiritual way and that just made a real sense to me, especially the life I lived, some kind of way to live your life, having a goal or path.

Q: You got injured in your fight against Cung Le, what happened?
Frank Shamrock: I got kicked in my forearm, and displaced my bone, actually it got broken - and to repair it they cut it open and put a plate in it and screws, and had to bolt it back together. I would like to fight him again. During the fight I didn't feel like I was in any danger, even with the broken arm I felt I could beat him.

Q: You were one of the first UFC fighters to get involved in TV and film work, what was it like working with Chuck Norris?
Frank Shamrock: I worked with Chuck Norris which was really amazing. I met him socially a few times and he invited me to be on his show. He is a very respectful and professional guy. I worked for 11 days on one of his episodes of 'Walker Texas Ranger' and it was absolutely amazing. It was some of the hardest days of work of my life, but some of the most gratifying as well. We did a show about a prison where the guards were running the inmates prison fights and putting them on the internet. Chuck and I starred in it and it was just a wonderful experience.

Also, I did a Burger King commercial. When I first started fighting in 1999 I went into acting and entertainment and I got a lot of offers for films and TV shows, and when the sport started growing again I got out of that and back in the sport to fighting more. I also did a couple of more films between now and then, one called 'No Rules'. I do a movie a year and a couple of commercials.

Q: You are one of the pioneers of the sport of mixed martial arts, what does the future hold for you?
Frank Shamrock: Pioneers of the sport are people like Royce Gracie, Ken Shamrock, Mark Coleman, Maurice Smith; they all made a huge impact on the sport when it was very young and really misunderstood. Some of them were artists and others were artists in their own way. Some guys were there trying to adapt and made a huge impact. I think there are a lot of guys who made the sport what it is today.

One of my focuses recently have been to spread the martial arts word and this is something which is important because martial arts is what made me who I am today. And for me to be able to share that with other people, it's huge for me. I plan on fighting more; I love fighting and feel I've got 10 more years left in me. I love being a martial artist professionally so I want to keep doing that as long as possible; from the teaching, training and fighting. I think it's the greatest life any one can ask for.

Q: What do you say to people who have misunderstood the sport of mixed martial arts. It feels as though they need to be educated and look beneath the surface before making comments?
Frank Shamrock: Again, you hit it on the head; it's a lack of education. I say, "You know what? Watch the show and meet some of the fighters, because you can't make a decision on it on what you hear or even by seeing one fight." I don't go around judging religious words and commenting on them because I don't know anything about it and why they are doing it, this is a good example.

BJ PENN
'THE PRODIGY'

BJ 'Prodigy' Penn was born and raised in Hilo, Hawaii and was the first non-Brazilian grappler to win the World Mundial Championships. At the age of 17, the young scrapper began training in Brazilian Jiu-Jitsu and had great success at competitive level.

He is one of only two UFC champions to have held the belt in two separate divisions - lightweight [155lbs limit] and welterweight [170lbs], the other being Randy Couture. Penn has been ranked the number 1 lightweight fighter in the world.

He is one those fighters who will fight anybody the UFC puts in front of him as he proved in some classic duels with Matt Hughes, Georges St Pierre, Jens Pulver and the highly controversial fight at UFC 84 with Sean Sherk. However, as one of the most down to earth fighters you could ever hope to meet, the Hawaiian readily admits that he is one of UFC's biggest fans. BJ Penn undoubtedly has a good future in the sport of mixed martial arts as he continues to dominate the competition.

Q: BJ, how did you get involved in the martial arts?

BJ Penn: A guy named Tom Callos, who was a martial arts instructor, moved about five houses from my house in Hawaii and he needed some people to wrestle around with and train Jiu-Jitsu with. He kept bugging my dad and asking him to send me to train with him but I didn't want to go. He kept bothering me, so one day my dad said to me, "Just go down once and you won't have to go anymore." So I went down and ended up liking it. Before that I was just doing some boxing for fun with friends and people all round town, all the time.

Q: How would you describe your teenage years growing up in Hawaii?

BJ Penn: At that age I was hanging out with friends and getting into street fights. A local street fighter named Saul, who was fighting all the time, he's been an influence to me.

Q: Let's talk about your competitive career before you pursued the UFC?

BJ Penn: I entered many jiu-jitsu tournaments, including going to Brazil and became a world champion in Brazilian Jiu-Jitsu. When I trained with Tom Callos, he introduced me to Ralph Gracie in California who became my instructor. Then I moved back to Hawaii and started training with a few instructors. Ralph was very good. I trained with a lot of different training partners, and trained with everybody from Frank Shamrock, Randy Couture, the 'American Kickboxing Academy' and Rigan Machado. It was awesome working with all these people; training with guys like that really helped me learn fast. You have to see what the best people do.

Q: Can you recall when you first saw the UFC?

BJ Penn: When I first saw the UFC I was around 13 or 14 years old. I thought it was cool! It was like real fights, but I wasn't really that interested in it. I liked to watch Royce Gracie. At the time it was cool and I wanted Royce to win and would cheer for him, but I was more into boxing at the time. The Gracies definitely revolutionised the martial arts and opened the doors for mixed martial arts.

Q: How did you get involved in the UFC?
BJ Penn: I knew Dana White from before I got involved in the UFC because I trained with him one time because John Lewis introduced me to him. After that I talked to Dana and asked him if he could get me into the UFC and eventually he got me in.

Q: Do you remember your first fight in the UFC and what did it feel to be fighting in the octagon for the first time?
BJ Penn- I fought George Gilbert and I was really pumped up and excited. It was kind of proving to myself that I'm a good fighter and I can fight with people who train for fighting. This was my favourite fight. To me, all my fights represent certain danger, whether it's against a kick-boxer, wrestler or a huge person; it's all equal. A fight is a fight; I'm willing to do everything to win the fight. 20 minutes before a fight I think about the game plan and techniques I'm going to use.

Q: Would you say you are an all-round fighter even though your base is Brazilian Jiu-Jitsu?
BJ Penn: It's very important to be an all-round fighter in mixed martial arts. You have to be good at striking, grappling and takedowns.For self-defence, jiu-jitsu is enough, but for MMA you need everything. I train as hard as I can all year round and whenever I get tired, I take time off. I cover everything from jiu-jitsu, boxing, kickboxing, wrestling. Conditioning also plays a huge part of my training regime. I do everything you possibly can think off from running, weights, calisthenics, bag work and so on. You need to find what the most important element you need to add to your game as far as specific schedule, sit down and figure it out.

Q: You beat Matt Hughes and lost to him, can you talk me through these fights?
BJ Penn: I felt good and I was in great shape. I was strong mentally and I don't just remember coming out but, as soon as I got in the fight I knew I was confident, I was going to win the fight. Everything just came together. It ended up him going to the ground and I ended up landing a good punch and choking him. It was over! I was really happy and very fulfilled. The hard journey was worth it in the end. In my rematch with him I did get hurt during the fight, I don't really want it to be some excuse but Hughes won that day. A defeat motivates me to train harder.

Q: In 2004, you started fighting in other arenas what was the experience like?
BJ Penn: It was just different in terms of place and events. The whole feeling is pretty much the same, you go there and go to the arena and warm up and fight. As far as I know, they were all the same. Fighting in Hawaii was easy because of the same time zone and the same climate, I felt very comfortable. There's a lot of MMA schools in Hawaii now and MMA is the biggest sport now in Hawaii.

Q: In your opinion how would a professional boxer do in a MMA fight?
BJ Penn: I would think a boxer would do good in MMA, but he's got to learn wrestling and jiu-jitsu to survive. When you see the guys in MMA standing and exchanging blows, the only reason they are boxing is they have not hit the ground yet. The weaker person on the ground is going to be taken down.

Q: In your view, what makes the sport of MMA so profound and exciting?
BJ Penn: I think everyone now understands it. You don't have to explain the rules to anyone because they know what's going on in the fight.

Q: How would you differentiate between an MMA fight and a street fight?

BJ Penn: There are differences, but the main thing is they also have similarities like elements of punching, kicking each other and slamming each other down. Of course, in street fighting you can do anything you want because there are no rules or rounds. Mixed martial arts and street fighting are two different things, you have two different attitudes; in a street fight, you get mad - I'm sure it happens in MMA but it really is a sport with rounds. I've had my share of street fights but I'll never get in trouble any more. When you fight in the ring or spar in MMA conditioning is important. In day to day self-defence, technique is important because it's not always going to be a long fight in the street.

Q: If you could change anything in the UFC what would it be?

BJ Penn: I would put kicks, knees and stomps on the ground and legalise kicking to the head of a grounded opponent.

Q: You fought outside of America in places such as Japan, how do you see the sport of MMA growing in the future?

BJ Penn: I think it's grown! The sport is going to grow huge in Europe and the U.K. and, everywhere in the world, it will get bigger. Without a doubt, mixed martial arts fighters should be making more money, it will turn that way. Everybody used to watch other sports, a lot of people are now turning to reality shows, now we have shows like 'Cops' and more realistic things. Mixed martial arts is a realistic sport and a sport for the new generation. My experience of the Ultimate Fighter was that it was very busy and tough and I had a great experience just being on the television show and seeing how it was filmed and the interaction with all of the people on the show. I had a great time and it really helped promote the UFC. I was in Afghanistan not long ago to visit the troops, the UFC sent us over. Michael

Bisping was there too, it was cool. I think the sport's grown to what it is now and it's just amazing.

Q: Do you have any comments on your victory over Sean Sherk?
BJ Penn: He got in and took me down, it was just a boxing match and I felt I was catching him with some good punches - and then I finally got to hit him with the knee and then caught him a with a couple of punches and it was over. I met [WWE star] 'The Rock' for the first time, he was in the audience, I'm a big fan of his.

Q: Sean tested positive for steroids; what are your feelings of athletes in the UFC taking these performance enhancing drugs?
BJ Penn: I think it's cheating and wrong! I think they're cowards! I don't think it's putting a bad reputation on the sport, but it's cheating and they shouldn't be doing it.

Q: What do you do to relax and recuperate?
BJ Penn: Recuperation is very important. I just try to go out and have fun. Just do whatever; go anywhere, travel, beaches, different islands and try to relax myself. I try to eat the most healthy and natural food when I'm training for a fight and try to stay away from the bad food.

Q: Is there any particular fighter you would like to fight?
BJ Penn: I will fight whichever fighter my fans want to see me fight in the biggest fight. I have ten years left in me, fighting pro. Our sport will no doubt surpass boxing. I don't know about other lightweight fighters, but I want to fight the best out there and the biggest names and put on a good show. I want to try my best and become a champion. In MMA I like watching all the fighters and I'm a fan of everybody, all the good guys.

Q: Anything you would like to add before concluding the interview BJ?

BJ Penn: My website is www.bj.com, I have a book out and another book coming out soon. I want to thank all the fans; no fans, no sport.

JENSPULVER
'LIL EVIL'

Jens 'Lil Evil' Pulver was born in Sunnyside, Washington and was raised in what he referred to as a 'Daily Hell'. His abusive father, who was a licensed horse jockey, was an alcoholic who would regularly dish out punishment to his children. Spurred on his experiences, Pulver got involved with wrestling at a competitive level before making a transition into the mixed martial arts arena.

After fighting in various MMA events, he was spotted by UFC matchmaker John Peretti. Pulver began competing in the UFC in 1999 and later became the first UFC lightweight champion. He has also fought in 'Pride' and WEC, which is owned by the UFC. Pulver is a colourful character, his rough upbringing and the hardships he had to endure and his life long struggle with depression is inspiring to anyone who wants to overcome obstacles and make a success of themselves. He continues to fight in MMA to this day and remains a match for almost anyone in the featherweight division.

Q: Jens, you had an extremely tough childhood where you went through hell when you were growing up, tell me more about this?

Jens Pulver: Yeah, when I was growing up it was tough. I was the eldest; I had 2 brothers and a sister, who is 8 years younger than me, who was a little too young to be in the middle of it all. My parents were young, 20 years old when I was born and it was real hard with the abuse, drugs and alcohol around us. My entire life growing up was one of those things, when I was a kid I went out and I used to think to myself when I come home my mother might be dead. Anywhere I stayed, at my friend's house and a lot of the times I could hear her screaming my name when I was five or six years old; she was kind of taking a beating with her. At least when he [my father] was beating me he wasn't beating the others. This has kind of been my rule, a family theme where I didn't want anyone else to get beat. Soon as he moved past, you moved out of the way, and he did what he did.

Q: Is it true that your father went as far as actually placing a gun in your mouth when you were as young as 7?

Jens Pulver: It's true; my mom actually told the story later on. It was one of those things when I was younger, and what I remember more than anything was being lined up and being scared. I knew it was a gun, but more than anything I'd seen, because I was too young. I remember him going out, saying he was going to kill himself and later coming back and talking with my mom. She explained everything. So, I guess at some point my body just kind of went elsewhere - it froze. When my mom brought that story alive in a book, I pretty much remember exactly what had happened. I never sat back and really delved back on it as I was growing up, but I do remember him few times going out telling us he was going to kill himself and then coming back and beating my mother up. So yes, that story is true.

Q: You graduated from Boise State University in criminal justice. Did your rough childhood have any impact on your education?

Jens Pulver: I went towards the direction I wanted; I really wanted to do wrestling. The truth was, in school I was never a serious student but you had to make grades Bs and Cs in order to do well in school, that's what kept me going. I always wanted to be able to wrestle, which I did in junior high school and college. When my wrestling career ended I went for the college degree. I went to college and graduated and then went into MMA, so it wasn't one of those things coming out of high school and finishing, I went to college and got my masters but I never expected to be a fighter for the rest of my life.

Q: Why did you start fighting in unsanctioned underground MMA fights?

Jens Pulver: Well, they weren't sanctioned because No Holds Barred was not legally sanctioned as a sport. UFC was on pay-per-view and cable and everybody was watching it. I fought with the intention of making a video tape. In high school gyms, we got in the boxing ring or a wrestling ring, we weren't sanctioned because nobody really knew what to call it. It wasn't even considered a sport. I just fought wherever I could fight so that I could get a video tape made more than anything else, so I can send the tape in and try to get in shows like 'Extreme Challenge,' which I had read about over time when I first started MMA, this was one of the big shows out there at the time.

Again, if you are not getting paid for fighting it goes under amateur rules, so there is no sanctioning body. We didn't have the gloves that you see in the UFC today, but they looked like them. I think they were called Boxer-genics. The first time I ever fought in an MMA fight, I just took my t-shirt off and went out into the arena and got the guy down and was able to get him in a rare naked choke. It was different!

Q: Do you remember watching the early UFCs when Royce Gracie was beating bigger guys, and did this inspire you in any way?

Jens Pulver: Yes it inspired me. He was winning his fights, but I've always believed in wrestling and I had the street fighting mentality to go with it. I was always in great shape. How many people on the street are in that kind of good shape? I mean, I can wrestle for two hours and go all day long and outlast the other guy. And when the ground fighting was brought to the attention of us, that's what gave me hope. I always wanted to be a boxer but the reality is when I'd seen mixed martial arts I said to myself, "You know what? This is it!"

I thought it's good to do boxing and I was wrestling growing up, and thought if we had something like punches and grappling put together It'll be a different outcome in a fight. When MMA came about that's what made the whole fighting thing great, and when I saw Royce Gracie out there doing what he was doing I was all excited about it. Then fighters like Pat Miletch and Randy Couture started to get into it all, and all the wrestlers I grew up watching came out and started competing too, that was the direction I wanted to go.

Q: You started training with Pat Miletch and Monte Cox took you under his wing. Is it true you packed your bags and flew out with only 200 dollars in your pocket?

Jens Pulver: I didn't have 200 dollars; I had a bunch of change! I had two bags with me when I came to stay with Monte; I had my wrestling and training attire in one and my personal clothing in the other bag. I got my first UFC fight before I even went out there. So I went out there to test my skills and it ended up with a draw. But I knew then that I was hooked. I had met Monte and Pat on the plane when we were flying out to one of the UFC's, this is when I knew what I wanted to do in my life. At the time, I was talking to Bob Shamrock a lot and he called Monte Cox and said, "I've got this guy you really should take him in."

Monte remembered who I was from the UFC and said he would absolutely, so I was extremely excited. I had no idea how cold it was going to be when I arrived in Monte's town. My mom packed me a big pack of lunch and I rationed it for two-and-a-half days. I wrote down all the goals what I wanted do and achieve when I got over here. I gave up everything, I still don't know where all that stuff is, it's gone. It's kind of like I had to say goodbye to that in order to live the last 10 years of my life of MMA.

Q: You became the first UFC lightweight champion when you beat John Lewis. Is it OK to tell me more about this?
Jens Pulver: What happened was, John Lewis had stepped onto the scene,   John Peretti, who was the match maker at the UFC, was the referee at the 'Bas Rutten Invitational' event, and it was here where I had a bunch of fights. Peretti noticed me and decided to give me a title shot. He always had this goal which was to start a lighter weight division in the UFC. People used to say to me that if I wanted to get into the UFC I had to get up to 170 pounds and I said, "No, I'll just keep knocking people out and beating them up.

I believe we both weighed in at 150 pounds, but still under the 170 division and this kind of started the talk for the weight thing. Then they kind of started making it more official. When John Lewis fought me, he had two guests with him on the day, it was Dana White and Lorenzo Ferrita. I went out there and knocked John Lewis out in 14 seconds, and when they took over the UFC they went out and got Caol Uno, and they wanted the number 1 guy and got me to fight for the belt. This was the first ever lightweight title.

Q: Your fight with BJ Penn is considered one of the highlights of your career. As I understand, you both disliked each other?

Jens Pulver: The first fight I had with BJ Penn, I remember at the time I had already defended my belt twice. And at the time, Frank Shamrock was talking BJ this and BJ that, and how BJ is the greatest thing, so that's really what got that rivalry going. I was the champion, but then when I watched him fight, "Oh my," he knocked out Caol Ono in the head in 12 seconds, and he beat Joe Gilbert and Din Thomas too.

I was like, "Good God, look at this!" So for the first fight against BJ at UFC 35, I was a big underdog, 6 to 1 underdog going into that fight. That had me fired up and motivated because although I was the champion I was the underdog, so it was a big fight. Going into the fight, it was close, in the second round he almost had that arm bar on me but I didn't tap and the time was up. I just never gave him that opportunity to be on top because I knew he could be extremely dangerous.

Then five years passed and people would always ask when the re-match was going to be, and I know BJ was up to 200 pounds. Then I came back and they wanted to put the fight on, which would be in the lightweight division in the 'Ultimate Fighter' series, so BJ and I would be the coaches. There was bad blood between us and it changed to a brawling theme. We were on the show for seven-and-a-half weeks and we were really mad at each other at that point.

Then going into the fight, BJ did a good job, I got out of the first round he got on top and again I made it tough, scored shots and takedowns, and I spent the second half on top. I knew, and the corner knew that he's going for a takedown, this time he didn't go for a submission which I was hoping for. He kept his position and kept throwing punches, that's when I knew I was in trouble, and he got that rare naked choke on me and that's when I had to tap.

Q: You began competing in pro boxing and won all your four fights. Why did you make this transition?

Jens Pulver: After I left the UFC, the first time I gave up the belt, I thought MMA wasn't that big like we see it today, so I made the decision to leave. I had this time on hand now so I thought I might as well use this time to really better all my skills. So, what better than sparring guys every day or I can go and start boxing? Whether or not it was for 600 dollars when you first start off boxing, I put myself in that scenario where you have that atmosphere and crowd and the thrill of fighting somebody you don't know.

I never expected my pro debut to be on ESPN, sure enough I was on ESPN on Tuesday Night Fight. It was just a way to keep me going and really work on my other skills. People can work on them all day long, talking to the coach and working the pads, but you're just not going to get the same kind of effect unless when you are going up against someone you don't know, and get that atmosphere. That's really why I took this direction, to stay active. I even did a couple of grappling matches.

Q: Now that you've boxed professionally what are your opinions on heavyweight boxing champions who were previously labeled as the world's toughest guys?
Jens Pulver: Well, I always say this; boxing and MMA are two different things. I know Muay Thai fighters and MMA guys who can sit back and break the boxer down. But what I learned from boxing is, like any sport or in a domain where you are only allowed to punch, using one method, some people can do an amazing job mastering the craft. Look at Mayweather, the guy's a gift. A guy like Ali or someone with the power of Mike Tyson.

I look at it like this OK, if the boxer does not train knees, clinches, takedowns, elbows, and punching is all he has in his arsenal then all he's going to concentrate on is punching his opponent. It's amazing what some people can do. I think hardcore MMA fans realise who focus on boxing that when you appreciate when you see a great boxer you have to stand back and go, "Good God." It's a very good sport and to be that good, that's an amazing thing to do. There's no comparison on the two.

Could a boxer beat this MMA fighter? No! If that boxer went and became an MMA fighter and he got really good as he was a boxer then he'd be disgusting [lethal]. But, if he is only a boxer then, no. But if you go in his world, now could an MMA fighter fight a boxer in a boxing match? Let's take Mayweather for instance, tell him to go over there and fight BJ Penn or someone! Mayweather may have some chance and BJ will obviously get him down and beat him, strike him and submit him.

But now its BJ's turn to go into the boxer's world, now you have to go out there and go six rounds with him in boxing; that's going to be the worst day of your life. He's going to hurt you bad. So you have to have appreciation for what boxing is, it's an amazing art when it comes to just using your hands.

Q: You returned to UFC 63, what was it like to be back in the octagon?
Jens Pulver: I never thought after being gone for three-and-a-half years that I would ever be back, and that was just an amazing honour for me. I sat back watched, Robbie Lawler, Kendal Grove, Matt Hughes was on top level, he was destroying GSP. When I was going to get that chance to come back in the UFC, when the time came, the walk down in the ring says it all. I had a smile on my face and I'm laughing and waving to every single person in the crowd. It was just great being back. I was never caught up in the moment that I was fighting, the fight wasn't important to me, the fact that I made it back and I was fighting back in the UFC in the octagon that was important to me, that fight was nothing.

Q: Do you believe hard work, effort and suffering have to

be endured to be successful in this world? What is your philosophy in life?

Jens Pulver: As far as fighting goes, the biggest thing is always the conditioning, hard work is definitely there. When I'm watching and learning more than anything to get in shape is one thing, and to move with the sport and get good at your craft and all your weak areas is another. That's what's amazing about watching a guy like Georges St Pierre and Anderson Silva, even BJ Penn in his last fight. This guy just hit him so deadly in every facet of the game, and at that point it will come back to conditioning.

It's hard to be able to focus on your conditioning which takes a lot of time and, at the same token, you have got to work on the elements that got you there, and develop some things that will help you progress and get better in fighting. Now you see people who are good at everything because they've been training long enough and the sport has been here for longer. Conditioning is still the biggest part. I don't care who you are; Bruce Lee or Muhammad Ali, if you're out of shape it doesn't matter after a minute you ain't that fast, you ain't that good . But after developing the conditioning then what do you do? Can you evolve to be an exceptional fighter out there in the same process?

Q: What has been the biggest battle in your life??

Jens Pulver: For me the biggest battle, first of all I have to say that fighting and training has been the best part. Battling with myself and dealing with the pain of growing up and allowing myself to be happy, allowing myself to know its OK and feeling positive. When something good is happening and you sit back and say, "Alright, when'sthe shoe going to drop, who's going to die, or somebody's going to get sick?"

Whenever I was happy we went and wrestled, but when we got home there would be nothing but the beatings and sadness. So that's been my biggest battle. I'm learning everyday that you have got to be positive and how to be a lot more calm. Instead of with my hairs up on my back waiting for that shoe to drop, I'm always expecting bad things to happen and never really allowed myself to enjoy what I'm doing. So that's been my greatest battle. I've never been afraid to admitting it to anybody. The fighting part is a blessing, to fight in MMA and do what I love doing and to be able to meet the fans every day, this has been the greatest part ever.

But to go home afterwards and get stuck, fear and it's like paranoia, the damages that happened to me and not allowing myself to have fun and enjoy myself. I don't drink, or do drugs, I'm not a violent person, but I'm bad on myself because I beat myself up with constantly being having fear anxiety attacks and worry. Even Monte gets a kick out of it as he teases me some times. I just freak out for no reason as I sometimes I think "God, this is going to happen and I'm not going to make it." I'm waiting for bad things to happen to me all the time.

Q: Some UFC fighters have had childhoods parallel to yours, on the other hand, a lot of them have college degrees and are educated people. How do you compare the two?

Jens Pulver: Everybody thought you had to be a delinquent drunk punk, straight from the bar stool into the octagon and people used to think we had to be punks because it was like your everyday fighting in the street. No, its not. Now people have started to understand it's a sport. I don't fight in the street; I haven't been in a street fight for 10 or 11 years. I have got no need. Like I said, I don't drink and I don't go in the bars. I went to college and got a degree. MMA is not about going out there and beating somebody up, this is my sport to test myself against another opponent.

My opponent came into it freewill to the sport and he's going to work on his skills. This is what we do. Some people are good at books, some at maths, some can fix cars. What I'm good at and love doing more than anything is working on skills; boxing, kicking, punching and being in shape and entertaining people. Now it's just a lot bigger world of fighters and more fans and people are starting to understand now that this isn't human cockfighting. The fighters don't have to come from a prison background or abused lifestyle to want to do this as a sport. It's definitely turned a full circle in way the people viewed the UFC in the beginning.

Q: Cub Swanson accused you of faking an injury because he felt you didn't want to fight him. What have you got to say on this subject?

Jens Pulver: The injury happened a week and a half before we were supposed to fight. I was disappointed. I have the doctor's report and the x-rays. Then I get this guy tell me this, after all the wars I've lived through and everything I've been through, all the people I've fought who I said I'd always fight. I'd said I'd fight anybody they'd put in front of me so he's got to be dumb enough not to remember who I am and tell me I'm going to pull out of the fight because I'm scared. The first thing that came into my mind was, "You know how much money I make? I'll tell you what, it's a hell lot more than you think if you think I can miss a fight!"

I'm a 145 pounder, they don't make that kind of money. I'm not making Chuck Liddell or Randy Couture cash. I'm not making cash what heavyweights make, period. I haven't fought for six figure sums ever in my life. So that had me mad and made me realise sitting here talking to my fiancée Konika, this guy's forgotten what I've done for the sport and he's exactly the person who's got to learn and he's going to learn quickly. So this is what really started that war and got me fired up, but also got me to back to where I needed to be; which is training and fighting.

Q: You have two books out and it seems you have a really

fascinating story to tell..

Jens Pulver: The book 'Little Evil' - One Ultimate Fighter's Rise to the Top', I have no idea about that book as far as where to get it from. I remember writing it a long time ago with a buddy of mine who co-wrote it with me, his name is Eric Krause. This was long time ago, I know they stopped printing copies about three years ago, I don't know where you can find the book. I've not seen a penny from it, I don't even know how to get a hold of these people [the publishers], they won't give back the rights, God knows, whatever. The book itself is a timeline, it goes through my childhood up to the BJ Penn fight. The other book, 'Never' which is written by a friend of mine is the book I love. This book is more of the mental side of me whilst being in MMA and it's pretty cool. It's about the conflicts and religious groups, I would say the book isn't all about me but most chapters cover me. It talks about moments with Matt Hughes, Tim Sylvia, Pat Milletch, Monte Cox, these people who have been around me and in this group, that's why I love the book 'Never, it's an amazing story.

Q: It seems you love to compete, where does this thirst of competing stem from?

Jens Pulver: Well wrestling really saved my life, literally saved my life. I wouldn't have a college degree, plus I didn't need a 2 .7 [grade average] in order to wrestle. The will to compete kept me in school and kept me in on the right path. If people don't believe me then I'll tell you, I have my brother who is serving 55 years in prison and he and I are only a year apart, and he just went on a different road. The reality for me is also on the other side, here is my dad beating us, beating me and telling me I'm a piece of shit, I'm never going to make it, I'm a bastard and a loser just like my mother so on so forth.

But here are all these coaches showing me that if you go out and put all the hard work and train your butt off and stay focused, then you'll be successful. If people are going to be positive you're going to feel it. The amount of gratitude I got from that by hearing praises from coaches and other athletes, it was a big scale tipper. I mean here I was in-between, I was on a fine line the whole time, my dad in a big city beating me up on one end and on the other hand the positivity and the amazing feelings I got from competing.

Really, this MMA is just adding punches in the world I've already known. I've been through one-on-one combat, I love the idea of one on one. I could be in a team of 11 people and I might go train hard, I might stay focused on the pads but the other 10 guys might be out drinking, screwing, whoring or whatever they do, and then we go out and lose - that's what I love, one on one competition.

If I have a broken heart, if I go in there out of shape then that's going to show. If you go out that way then, this will fall back on you and there's nobody to turn to but yourself. I loved it that way, that's what shaped me and training and being around the coaches, one day being able to be in a position that I'm moving towards now just turn around and help kids who were walking in my shoes before. Turn around and tell them, "This is what I did, and this is what you can do". That is going to be my job when I'm ready to retire from the sport, I'm going to move in with the full circle become a coach as the coaches saved my life.

Q: We hear you're a big video games fan.
Jens Pulver: Oh I love games. I don't know where it comes from but, for me, I love the graphics and I love the styles of certain games. I'm not going to grab a gun or be in a war or jungle, or fighting and shooting other people, that's not going to happen in my life ever. But I can simulate and play on the video games and the feeling's are there. I've always loved playing computer games.

Q: Was your last fight for WEC?

Jens Pulver: I fought on June 1st for the World featherweight title and lost to a 5-round decision. It was voted one of the fights of the year and the organisation was WEC - which is the same owners of UFC. We sold out the arena, broke records as far as how many tuned into view the fight, and that's great because the co-main event was 145 pound and 135 pound fights. That was an amazing event.

Q: UFC is beating boxing in certain respects and filtering into the mainstream. How do you feel about the enormous success of MMA?
Jens Pulver: The reason its beating boxing is because for one, a lot of those top fighters in boxing for a long time wouldn't fight each other. You finally started seeing the 142 , 146 pounders, such as Ricky Hatton, Sugar Ray Mosley, you started seeing big matches like that. Right now, MMA is the biggest thing because the guys who want to fight are not only good with their hands but you don't have to be good with just with your hands, you can be good at grappling, wrestling, kicking.

So right now, in this sport we always ask the question like, "Have you seen Mike Tyson do his thing"? and then, "Have you seen this great wrestler do his thing?" and if those two met I wonder what would happen. MMA came along and answered those questions, and this is the front runner for combative sports.

Q: When are you fighting next?
Jens Pulver: There's no official news but I would like to fight as soon as possible. I'm waiting and sitting back just waiting for the official send out the agreement, and I sign it and I want to fight as soon as possible. I want to get back on the horse again and I want another shot at Urijah Faber. I want to fight him again and go out there and take my fight and earn my rematch. I'm still under the same umbrella WEC owned by the UFC.

Q: What are your future plans?
Jens Pulver: I have a daughter who I want to see grow up and my wife Konika is pregnant with our baby. Future for me personally, is to have a family and be the opposite father that I had. Fighting-wise I want to fight as soon as possible and I think I've shown people I'm not done yet. I'm not retiring and still ranked the number four guy in the world. Really, right now, man, the future is wide open. God knows, I'm after this fight hopefully in December.

Q: Were you influenced by Bruce Lee?
Jens Pulver: You know what, I was influenced by him. Because of his size, he's a little guy out there doing his thing and this gave me hope. I was in one of those positions where I was too big to be small. My parents were jockeys and I spent my whole life up till I was 15 preparing to be a jockey. I was going to ride horses and that was what I was going to do as a career, but then I got too big and heavy but I was too small and not big enough to do anything else.

Bruce Lee gave me hope because he was my size, his speed and flexibility alone, if I can have that alone, oh my God, absolutely I was influenced by him. I wasn't a big practitioner of the martial arts but I was a practitioner of his discipline and style of Bruce Lee. The way he thinks, the way he trained, the way he focused on it and the way he believed in himself and slept, ate and drank his art and that was very influential.

Q: Do you think Bruce Lee was one of the first martial artists who opened people's eyes to investigate and evolve?
Jens Pulver: I think he's one of the reasons why mixed martial arts came about, absolutely, because people had that question. This guy was fast, he'd kick you six times in the face before your eyes could see him do the first kick. How are you going to beat him? So that started really the question… and in order to defend that, some of the people he competed against comparing

their style people brought that to him. What if I grab a hold of you, you've got to figure something out. I think that's what really started the revolution of that question; what if a guy on the ground grabs a hold of somebody, let's find out how to deal with it.

VITOR BELFORT
'THE PHENOM'

Vitor 'The Phenom' Belfort is the youngest UFC heavyweight champion in history. He won this coveted title at the age of 19 in 1997. Born and raised in Rio de Janeiro's notorious crime-infested neighbourhoods, Belfort started martial arts training so he could defend himself and developed a healthy appetite for competition.

He became one of Carlson Gracie's top students and fighters. At the age of 18 he moved to the US to compete in MMA professionally. Some of the toughest fights of his career have been with such elite fighters as Randy Couture, Chuck Liddell, and the controversial defeat to Tito Ortiz.

Belfort is known to a have some of the fastest hands in UFC history, a fact which he demonstrated against Wanderlei Silva when he knocked the 'Axe Murderer' out with a combination of chain punches at 'UFC Brazil' in October 1998. He also once held the Cage Rage light-heavyweight title, before parting ways with the organisation in 2007. He presently fights for 'Affliction' organisation and makes his homes in Brazil and the US.

Q: Vitor, what was it like growing up in Brazil?
Vitor Belfort: I grew up in Brazil, when I was really young, I was a professional volleyball player and I really liked sport. I also used to play soccer and tennis. I grew up in a neighbourhood which was a tough neighbourhood and it was all about survival. Fighting in the street was common and we had to defend ourselves. I started to do martial arts to protect myself. I was four years old when I started doing judo; then, when I turned 13, I started Brazilian Jiu-Jitsu and at 14 I started doing boxing as well.

When I turned 15, I made a decision that I wanted to do Vale Tudo. In the city where I lived, there were regular robberies and street crime, I didn't want to look like a punk with people robbing me and making fun of me, so I started doing martial arts, and this really helped me. I never like violence, but I like the sport of fighting. Many people in Rio de Janeiro try to take advantage of other people so I started to do martial arts to protect myself and this helped me.

Q: Do you feel Brazil is much more dangerous than America?
Vitor Belfort: Yes, in Brazil there's more corruption, too much poverty and social problems. You will see people with the attitude like, "Why does that guy have a nice car and I don't have it", they want to have it too. I think there are less opportunities here in Brazil and the poverty is high which makes Brazil more dangerous than America for sure.

Q: When did you have your first vale tudo fight?
Vitor Belfort: I used to do Vale Tudo in the gym where I trained, people would come to the gym and they would fight. Back in those days it was martial arts style against martial art style; judo against jiu-jitsu, boxing against jiu-jitsu, to prove which martial art was effective. At the time when I was fighting, Carlson Gracie was my coach; we had a relationship like a father and a

son. He took me under his wing.

When I was 18 years old I fought in my first professional fight in Hawaii in the 'Superbrawl' tournament. I beat my opponent [Jon Hess] in 17 seconds. Back in those days they didn't have weight divisions, I was 190 pounds and my opponent was 300 pounds. He was very tough and really good. I gained experience and right after this fight, I went to fight in the UFC. They invited me to fight for the title in the heavyweight division, this was the time when the UFC had started doing weight classes. I fought in both the heavyweight and the light-heavyweight divisions. I fought two opponents on the same night and won the heavyweight title. I was the youngest UFC heavyweight champion ever at the age of 19. Nobody has broken this record to date.

Q: What did you think of Royce Gracie beating bigger opponents in the earlier UFCs?
Vitor Belfort: Royce was great, he proved that Jiu-Jitsu was the most effective martial art in the business, because if you don't know Jiu-Jitsu, you are going to have problems. Right now we have mixed martial arts, you can be the best boxer in the world, or the best wrestler in the world, but if you don't know Jiu-Jitsu you are going to be submitted and lose. I feel Jiu-Jitsu is one of the most effective fighting styles.

Q: What did you think of the cultural differences when you moved to America?
Vitor Belfort: The difference between the two countries is that America is the land of opportunity. In America, you have the opportunity to make it big in all sports. In Brazil, the only sport that gets you anywhere on the world stage is soccer. There aren't many opportunities for other sports. The good thing about America is that you can do anything. American people support whatever you do. I like the way they're professional and the opportunities that are available.

211

Q: What was your experience like fighting in Japan?
Vitor Belfort: I like Pride; it was a great experience. In Japan, the fans support the sport and there is a lot of respect for the fighters. The culture is different, but there are opportunities in the sport. I like it a lot, the fans there are more quiet, observant and different, they know the difference and they understand the sport technically. The sport is developed in Japan.

Q: UFC 46 you beat Randy Couture for the light-heavyweight title. What are your views on Randy and the fights you had with him?
Vitor Belfort: For me, he's one of the best fighters in the world. He's so nice as a person, a good fighter, good human being and it was wonderful for me to fight a guy like Randy. We had a total of three fights where he beat me two times and I beat him one time.

It was a good experience for me and he taught me a lesson in the first fight which was; never underestimate a fighter. Randy is the kind of a guy when he goes in the ring it doesn't matter if you are a better fighter than him he's going to make sure that he's going to stick to his game plan and he's going to fight you. He's not going to back up, but he's going to go forward and after you, and stick to his game plan. Randy is a perfect example, as a fighter and a coach. We are good friends and right now I'm training at his facility out of Las Vegas with his trainers. Randy has helped develop the sport of MMA, he's a very good man.

Q: When you fought Randy, your sister had been kidnapped, did this affect your mind set and performance in the fight?
Vitor Belfort: Yes sure, two weeks before the fight, my sister disappeared but I was so focused for the fight I wanted to be the champion of the world again. I was the champion of the heavyweight division and at the time I was fighting in the light-

heavyweight division. I got the call from the UFC telling me I didn't have to fight if I didn't want to, but I went and fought.

I won the belt, then Randy, in the rematch at UFC 49, won it off me. At that time, I was very out of focus and depressed because my sister was still not found. Randy was ready and focused mentally physically and spiritually, he got the belt and he deserved it, I was really out of focus. I think my strategy for this fight was not to go after him, he caught me with an elbow and a headbutt and I couldn't do anything. I got a cut and the referee stopped the fight.

We never know what could have happened if the referee didn't stop the fight. I like to think about that and see what could have happened but at the same time I don't want to take anything away from my opponent. Randy was very ready for the fight and beat me in the fight and he deserves it. So, that's how I see it. I'm the kind of a guy, I don't look back, but look at the future, so I learned my lesson; in MMA, anything can happen. You can never give the opportunity to your opponent, you have to make sure you have to dominate him from the beginning to the end. Randy dominated this fight and he deserved the win.

Q: When you fought Tito Ortiz in February 2005 you broke his nose. You lost via decision, just how disappointed were you?
Vitor Belfort: This fight with Tito was a big robbery. The judges robbed me so big and everybody knows; he knows, even his brothers in his corner know who really won the fight. The judges gave the fight to him, and we had a problem. I won the fight but I'd been cheated.

In the last round I got tired and he just lay on top of me and he didn't do anything, he was just trying to buy time. I'm ready to fight him again and I'll beat him again. I got mad with the UFC; I was really disappointed with the decision. Back at the time Tito was a big name, it was a big upset and I was very disappointed. I think Affliction are going to put the fight on, because I think Tito is going to sign for Affliction soon. I think this will be a big fight for Affliction, to put that on pay-per-view and we're going to make millions and millions of pay-per-views because everybody wants to see the rematch. 'Vitor Belfort versus Tito Ortiz II', that would be a big fight.

Q: You demonstrated your hand speed against Wanderlei Silva; do you think you became known for having the 'fastest hands in the UFC'?
Vitor Belfort: Yes, I beat him. Wanderlei is a very tough fighter and this was a big fight for me. First of all I thank God for this gift, it's a gift given to me; the other thing is, I train hard. I fought in boxing amateur fights and then fought one professional fight. I have good hands and boxing skills so I tried to compete and train in boxing for a while.

Q: How did you find the experience of fighting in Europe on the Cage Rage promotion?
Vitor Belfort: They invited me to fight in Europe, so I did it to prove myself in Europe and treat it as another challenge for me. I fought in Cage Rage and won the championship and was really happy. I was undefeated there and won the belt, but they never gave the belt to me. I was disappointed with the organisation. That was totally unprofessional on their part and I just don't fight for them anymore because if they can't respect me as a fighter they will never respect me as a person.

I don't know why they didn't give me the belt, I beat the champion. When I called them to ask where my belt was they would said, "We've shipped it out, the belt is held in customs" - they always were lying to me. So, I thought these guys are lying to me and being very unprofessional. I'm not going to fight for them because you can't trust them. If you can't trust a person who is lying to you then you can never work for them. Right now, I'm very happy with Affliction,

ULTIMATE CONVERSATIONS: **VITOR BELFORT**

they treat me like a person.

Q: Do you feel Brazilians are some of the best mma fighters, is it the right time to get into MMA?
Vitor Belfort: Yes, this is the perfect time for Affliction we have the best card and fighters, so now we are going to keep growing. Everybody is going to be big, UFC is big and Affliction is going to be big; healthy competition is all good. I think now is the time.

Q: What has been the highlight of your career and which would you say has been your toughest fight so far?
Vitor Belfort: Every moment is good. Everybody, from fighting Randy Couture, Chuck Liddell and Heath Herring. Chuck is one of the biggest fighters in the UFC for sure. He's a good fighter and a very marketable fighter and he deserves it.

Q: Would you ever fight in the UFC again?
Vitor Belfort: Right now, I'm with Affliction; we have good fighters in Affliction, we are willing to fight with anybody, anybody with the belt we can challenge. We have good promoters at Affliction and its good for the sport and fans. The UFC has a lot of fighters too; everything is going to depend on co-promotion, so we are going to need UFC people to start a record of us. I'm a fighting man; I want to fight the champion. I just want to put on a good fight for the fans.

Q: How many more years are you going to be fighting professionally in MMA?
Vitor Belfort: I'm 31 years old, young and fresh and ready to fight again. I think MMA needs new promotions coming up like Affliction. Right now, it's a good time for the new promotions competing with the UFC which is good for the sport. I'm really proud of seeing this. The difference between the UFC now, compared to when I started 1997 is there's more opportunities

and money now.

Back in that time, there were no rules but now the sport is more organised; bigger promotions, bigger money and is more professional than before. I have two houses; I live in Brazil and US.

Q: Have you any comments to add?
Vitor Belfort:I want to thank the fans and thank the Lord to give me the opportunity to keep fighting; he's the reason why I'm alive. I want to also thank all the promoters. We have a reason in life, one of the reasons in life is to live right and work hard.

QUINTON JACKSON
'RAMPAGE'

Quinton 'Rampage' Jackson is a former amateur wrestler who turned to mixed martial arts after seeing the success of fellow amateur wrestlers in MMA. After a string of victories in shows such as King of The Cage and Danger Zone, Rampage went onto fight in Pride where several incredible performances catapulted him to stardom. During this time, he fought some elite fighters, namely Wanderlei Silva, Chuck Liddell, Igor Vovchanchyn and Kazushi Sakuraba; only losing to Silva.

Rampage made his UFC debut at UFC 67, avenging an early career loss to Marvin Eastman with a savage knock out, which the high-spirited fighter jokingly referred to as 'Black-on-black crime' in his post fight interview. On May 2007 in UFC 71, he faced the then light-heavyweight champion, Chuck Liddell, and knocked 'The Iceman' out in the first round, clinching the title belt in the process.

Jackson coached a team of athletes on 'The Ultimate Fighter 7' series, alongside, 'TUF' series one winner, Forrest Griffin. At UFC 86, these coaches fought and after a grueling 5-round war, Griffin was able to wrestle the title from Rampage's clutches. He is now back in training, eyeing future opponents.

Q: What kind of a childhood did you have?
Quinton Jackson: My neighbourhood was very rough. We were street kids always hanging out; we drank alcohol, smoked weed and cigarettes, stole stuff out of the grocery stores like street punks. This all happened when I was growing up. There were street gangs around. We would go driving in stolen cars on the other side of town. My brother would get his ass beat because he would go mess with people, and I would have to go beat their ass, and after that I would beat his ass.

There were bullies who would bully my friends or my brother and I would fight the bullies. When I was a kid I used to get into fights, people gave me a nickname, 'Mike Tyson', because the way I used to try to knock out my opponent on his ass. I was more of the protector of my family and friends. So now I'm more of a fight celebrity fighting in the UFC and I have fans. I don't have a right to judge what kind of person anyone is, or someone like Kimbo Slice, but I'm glad he's in MMA and doing it legally. Everyone has their own choices to make, who's to say anything about anyone else. He's come into the sport now and I wish him the best. We're all the same in that we're professional fighters. I respect anyone who goes into the octagon and fight.

Q: Am I right in saying that you originally wanted to pursue a career in pro wrestling?
Quinton Jackson: When I was a kid I watched pro wrestling a lot. I'm from Michigan, where pro wrestling was very popular - and I thought I was going to be a pro wrestler, a stuntman or a fireman.

Q: You fought and beat Chuck Liddell twice - in Japan and the UFC. Do you have any comments on your battles with the 'Iceman'?
Quinton Jackson: I loved Japan! It was great. They had tough fighters in Japan and I learned a lot about fighting there. I

always fought under pressure, it helped me to become a better fighter. I fought really hard against Chick Liddell and my intention was t to win the whole tournament to show the world I'm the best fighter in the world. I beat Chuck and proved to the world I was the best fighter. My plan was to beat the hell out of Chuck and don't let anything stop me, and just whoop his ass.

Of course I beat him again in UFC 71 and proved to people the first victory wasn't a fluke. I knew I had to finish it quick... I had a small injury so I didn't want the fight to carry on for a long time, so it worked out perfectly, thank God.

Q: Would you like to fight him again?
Quinton Jackson: I wouldn't mind fighting Chuck again, but after his last fight, I don't think he's going to fight for a while. I hope he recovers and gets back into the octagon; he's an icon for the sport. And if he decides to fight, I'll be back to my best. It's good to see someone get knocked out in a fight, but it's bad for the fighter afterwards. Before I can even think about fighting Chuck, he needs to get back to the top form. I'll fight Chuck one more time too and I'll knock him out too.

Q: What is your friendship like with Tito Ortiz?
Quinton Jackson: Me and Tito have been friends for a long time and I look up to him. I go to the Big Bear mountain training facility to train, he's an icon for the sport. Tito has that X-factor. He's one of those guys you want to see; win or loose, everybody wants to see Tito fight. If you think about it a lot of fighters don't have that, only one percent of the fighters have that. Tito has that and I've got that, Michael Bisping's got that; you want to listen to what we have to say.

I like Chuck Liddell, but everybody just want to see him fight, nothing outside that. Fans of the sport want to see him in the octagon just fighting. But outside that it's different. But with Tito you want to see what he's doing and what he's saying. When he's done after the fight he has something to do or something to say, like the t-shirts he puts on after the fight.

Q: You don't watch UFC fights a great deal, do you?
Quinton Jackson: I don't watch it a whole lot, I'm just a weird person in my own little world. But I watch it when someone like GSP or Randy Couture fight. I want to see what Randy's going to do, whether he is going to knock the person out or submit him. He's an old guy but still going strong. I like to watch my friends, Michael Bisping and [Cheick] Kongo fight. I don't watch too many of my own fights but I'll watch them now and again. The UFC has made me more of a fan than I ever was when I was fighting in Pride to be honest.

Q: You're a spiritual person and embraced religion. What made you go this direction?
Quinton Jackson: My mom and grand ma were very spiritual, and when I was older I started to go to church. Now I'm a child of God and I try to be spiritual. God chose me to be in his kingdom. Spiritual thinking must not be misunderstood; like some other religious people who do the wrong things to use religion for their own wrong doings. I just want people to know that I'm a child of God and I'm happy with what I am. This has made me a better person, if it doesn't then there's something wrong with you.

Q: The much talked about Forrest Griffin fight was controversial, everybody knows it was. It seems Forrest did not share this view. What is your view?
Quinton Jackson: Forrest can say whatever he wants, but everyone else says it was a controversial fight. I watched the fight and I thought I won. Firstly, he just won the rounds, two and five in my eyes. You know what, the fans think so too. I don't care the fight's old news, but I think a bunch of fans should do a poll on what they think. He thought he lost too, so I don't know why he would say it's not controversial. I'll tell

you what, the next time I fight Forrest I'm going to be better prepared and in a better frame of mind and its going to be a lot better fight for Rampage, trust me. I lost respect for Forrest because he didn't think it was a controversial fight, everyone else thinks it was. The fight could have went either way because that's what happens in UFC, but by no means it should have been an unanimous decision.

Q: Now that you will be spending some time in the UK, what do you think of the UK scene?
Quinton Jackson: I love the UK! I'm coming out here and I can do my thing with less distractions, and it's cool. I like training with Michael Bisping and I'll train hard and get better. Michael is one of the hardest working fighters I've seen. I've had a lot of people before saying, "What are you doing joining the Wolfslair team?", and, "What you doing with the Bisping team, you're the champion!"

I'll tell you what, Michael Bisping is a good fighter and a lot of people around him are good and I can be a lot better fighter and sparring partner by working with these guys. I've come here a couple of times before and spent some time and was very impressed at what I saw. I think it's the best team on the planet, so I'm really happy here. I think the UFC is going to grow bigger all over the world. It's the fastest growing sport in the world. Some other people may make comments and criticise the sport, but we're not talking bad about any of the other sports, we put on good full contact fights, it's a great sport.

WANDERLEI SILVA
'THE AXE MURDERER'

Wanderlei Cesar De Silva was born in Curtiba, Brazil. After earning a name for himself in the No Holds Barred competitions of his native land, Wanderlei scored some unparalleled success in the Japanese promotion Pride, as he tore through a long list of over-matched opponents. The tough Brazilian dominated his division and earned the nickname of 'The Axe Murderer' because of his aggressive fighting style.

He has exceptional Muay thai and a black belt in Brazilian Jiu-Jitsu, making him one of the most well rounded fighters in the game. He made his UFC debut on October 16, 1998 and fought a couple times in the UFC before making a transition to Pride where he held the Pride middleweight championship belt. He sensationally returned to the UFC in December 2007, losing to Chuck Liddell in a hard fought match.

Silva recently moved to Las Vegas where he feels close to home, fighting in the UFC and continues to be a headliner. He is widely considered one of the toughest mixed martial artists to step in to a ring and octagon. He has a mild mannered approach outside the octagon, yet the heart of a champion, always ready to fight the best.

Q: What is your martial arts background?

Wanderlei Silva: I started training in Muay Thai at the age of 13, because I was fat when I was a kid, and I needed to lose weight; this is the reason why I started training. A year later, I had my first Muay Thai fight which I won in a mere 27 seconds. After this fight I stopped training. I started training in Brazilian Jiu-Jitsu and fighting in mixed martial arts later because there were no MMA events. My first MMA fight occurred when I was 20 years old.

Q: Just how popular is MMA in Brazil?

Wanderlei Silva: In Brazil, MMA is very popular, but there's too many fighters and too many events. The events don't pay a lot of money, it's very hard in Brazil because every fighter is a good fighter and they know all the techniques on the ground and are good strikers too, but there's not much TV coverage for MMA there. So it's hard to make a good living there in the sport, because there are less lucrative sponsorships compared to America.

Q: What do you think of the Gracies who popularised the No Holds Barred phenomenon?

Wanderlei Silva: Gracies are the creators of jiu-jitsu and the family is known around the world, they have good fighters. I think, me and every mixed martial arts fighter need to thank them, if we didn't have the Gracies, we wouldn't have had MMA. Royce is the best Gracie fighter; he fought the best guys who were real fighters, who were stronger and heavier than him. He's a very good fighter and I respect him a lot.

Q: Let's talk about your training, what elements do you integrate into your rigorous regime?

Wanderlei Silva: My training, basically, looks like this; physical conditioning in the morning and fighting in the afternoon. I include running, I train in jiu-jiitsu, wrestling, boxing, Muay Thai and MMA,every day is different. The guys who want to fight in MMA need to train in striking and grappling because you need to be a complete fighter, otherwise it's not possible to get to the top. You need to have a good trainer and a good gym and really perform well.

Q: Why did you make a decision to move to Las Vegas?
Wanderlei Silva: I moved to Las Vegas because the UFC company is based here; it's better for me and I have direct contact with the boss, my wife and brothers are here and it's very good here. There is more money and better promotion here in the US; there is more media exposure compared to anywhere else.

Hopefully, in the future, I would like to open my own gym and have more students. Fighters from Brazil are moving from Brazil to America, Europe and Japan because there's more exposure and money in the fight business in these countries. I'm also training with Randy Couture here in Las Vegas and he has a very good gym with some good professional fighters. Right now, I don't have my own gym here but one day I would like to open my own gym. Randy's Couture is a great guy and I have a good relationship with him, and he's very good for my training.

Q: How did you find fighting in Pride?
Wanderlei Silva: My first fight was in the UFC in Brazil with Vitor Belfort, and I was really disappointed when I lost the fight. But, then I went to Japan and won many times, it was really nice there - and my life changed. For seven years, I dominated my division, fighting the best guys and I became a champion. My name became bigger and my life really changed. I had a contract with Pride which was the biggest show and very popular in Japan. My fans loved me, I stopped working in my day job after I started fighting in Japan and I started training full time.

Before, I was fighting and working my day job, it was very hard I had no time to relax, all I did was train and go to work. After I started to fight in big promotion, I made more money and got more exposure. My first fights in Japan were not paying a lot of money. I was the world champion in my division - 205lbs division -and it was the best time in my career.

Q: Do you think fans in Japan are different to any other country?
Wanderlei Silva: Yes, the fans there love to see fights and the stadiums in Japan attract up to 100,000 fans. Here, in the US, 20,000 is the average turn out but the TV coverage is good. In Japan, the tickets are sold out two months before a fight, this is incredible.

In Canada every ticket sold out in just one day; a total of 22,000 tickets, it really is incredible. More and more fans want to see MMA now and the tickets are more expensive. In the US they go up to $300 or $400, but every ticket gets sold out here. This is great because more people are coming into the MMA fan base. Intime, MMA will be even more popular than it is now and in the US, it's made it on to the mainstream channel now. I think it's going to get bigger than boxing in the future.

Q: You fought Chuck Liddell at UFC 79 in a breath-taking match. You both were trying to box each other out. What are your comments on the fight?
Wanderlei Silva: Yes, the gloves are thin compared to the boxing gloves and it is very hard trying to box each other out. He was much taller and stronger with a strong punch. He was the UFC champion for five years and a really good fighter, and I was the champion in Japan. I gave him a good fight and maybe I would have a rematch with him in the future.

Q; Is there any particular fighter you would like to fight?
Wanderlei Silva : I would like to fight Quinton Jackson for the

belt and be a world champion again.

Q: You beat Keith Jardine at UFC 84, do you have any comments on this fight?
Wanderlei Silva: It was a big fight and he's in the top three in the rankings. He did surprise me and he's a good fighter.

Q: What is the difference between the Pride and UFC rules?
Wanderlei Silva: Basically, they use the kicks and knees in the face when the opponent is on the ground, in Pride. On the other hand, in the UFC all this is not possible. I like to use these techniques, but it's OK to fight with UFC rules. The ring in Pride is different to fighting in the cage. In the ring, I have a corner and I can talk to my cornermen.

Q: Which has been your hardest fight of your career so far?
Wanderlei Silva: Fight with Chuck UFC 79, my fight with Dan Henderson and the two fights with Quinton Jackson. I've had many tough fights during my career.

Q: Now that you have moved to the US what is the difference in lifestyle in Brazil and US?
Wanderlei Silva: Here, in the US, it's much more secure; in Brazil, it's too dangerous and there's too much violence, this is not good for me as I have a young son and a wife and my family. Basically, there is much more violent crime back in Brazil. In the US, there's much more promotion for the sport and good money, which is good for my career. I have good conditioning and if I'm injury free I have about 10 more fighting years left in me.

FORREST GRIFFIN

Forrest Griffin is best known for sensationally winning the light-heavyweight tournament in the first series of the extremely successful, 'The Ultimate Fighter' show. Over the course of three rounds which would prove invaluable to the development of the sport, Griffin and his teak tough opponent, Stephan Bonnar engaged in one of the most famous brawls in MMA history, in front of a record-breaking home audience.

Griffin graduated from the University of Georgia with a bachelor's degree in political science and served as a law and enforcement officer. Ironically, when he first saw the earlier UFC's, the American found them to be boring and barbaric. He made a U-turn when his Police defensive tactic instructor showed him a UFC tape featuring Randy Couture and Vitor Belfort; sparking Griffin's interest in MMA and sending him headlong into an impressive professional career.

Alongside Quinton 'Rampage' Jackson, Griffin was the coach on 'TUF' series 7 as the two fighters prepared to square off for the light-heavyweight title at UFC 86. After a close 5-round contest, Griffin fought claimed a well-deserved decision victory over Rampage to take possession of the championship belt. Griffin currently fights out of Las Vegas and is closely connected to former legendary UFC great Randy Couture's Extreme Couture team.

Q: You graduated with a bachelor's degree in political science, can you tell me what your educational background is and what interests you had growing up?
Forrest Griffin: Yes I did, I went to college just like anybody else and got a degree. I really liked international affairs and stuff like that. I enjoyed the usual sports and I played basketball and football.

Q: Why did you pursue a career as a police officer?
Forrest Griffin: There's two answers to why I became a police officer. The first one - which is true - is because I liked the idea of driving around for 8 or 12 hours and helping people out and getting paid to do this. Kind of, a Good Samaritan. To do stuff that you don't have any opportunity to do in another job and get paid to do that. And the second reason is, that I like to drive fast and to carry a gun and wear the uniform, and on top of this, getting free coffee. These are the two reasons why I became a cop!

Q: Did you witness any major incidents that you want to talk about?
Forrest Griffin: You know what, it wasn't as dangerous as I perceived it; there were no pistol shoot outs, actually I shot only once and hit a dear, which was pretty horrible. But, yes that's the only time I ever discharged my weapon. I didn't get to shoot that much back then. I don't think fighting is more dangerous than a cop's job, no one's died in the UFC.

Q: Is it true that your defensive instructor at the Police academy showed you a UFC tape and you thought it was boring?
Forrest Griffin: The first time I saw UFC was on a tape when I was actually in high school. I didn't really like it as I thought it was kind of boring and barbaric. Then when I was in the police academy when I was 20 years old, the defensive tactics

instructor had us do all the training stuff and I really liked the boxing and the wrestling and had fun with it and I loved it. He said, "You really love that UFC stuff". He knew I was doing some tough man contests at the time just for a laugh. I said the UFC looked kind of boring to me, so he gave me a UFC tape which featured Randy Couture who fought Vitor Belfort for the first time and that whole event was pretty good and professional, there were weight classes and it looked like a real sport and not just a barbaric fight with no rules.

Q: How would you then compare the UFC to the earlier No Holds Barred era when it first started?
Forrest Griffin: It's hard to compare that earlier era which had a lack of officialising and the lack of refereeing, lack of sportsmanship that you had back then compared to what we have now. But it's not that much safer now than it was in the no gloves days because the athletes are better now, they hit harder and they do their submissions harder, they are just better.

Q: How did you get involved with 'The Ultimate Fighter' show?
Forrest Griffin: Yes, that was kind of my break. I had actually given up on making it to the UFC before I got a call to be on the show. I thought it was great and a real good medium for the transfer of viewership, targeting people who wouldn't otherwise buy pay per views or, in the beginning, most people weren't interested as it was hard to get people to watch fights. I know for me, I always try to show people fights.

Q: UFC 49 you fought one of the all time greats Tito Ortiz?
Forrest Griffin: It was kind of my first experience on the big stage and I didn't do so well. There were a lot of factors that go into that fight but the biggest thing is just to keep my head...I, kind of, got a little star struck.

Q: What happened to you after the Keith Jardine fight at UFC 66, It seems you had an emotional breakdown?

Forrest Griffin: My thing has always been, if you never found something in your life that you were really passionate enough about to cry about, because you never felt that way towards something, and had a goal that you believed in that greatly...I kind of felt sorry for myself. You haven't experienced what you really like to be when you felt so passionate about something.

Q: Am I right in saying you wanted to fight Ken Shamrock?

Forrest Griffin: Yes, the situation behind that was, Tito Ortiz had hurt his knee and might not have been able to fight Ken Shamrock, and the fighters out here knew I was in good shape and I said I'd love to fight Ken Shamrock. But Tito Ortiz ended up being OK and ended up fighting after all.

Q: Tell me about your shoulder injury and any injuries you have sustained during your UFC career?

Forrest Griffin: I hurt my shoulder originally in 2001 in a fight in South Africa, it wasn't the same anymore and it hurt. And in the beginning of 2005 I kind of popped it out again where the shoulder joint actually came out - then it really got painful to do basic stuff like brush my teeth. This went on for a year! The thing is I hadn't fought for a while so I wanted to have at least one more fight before I did that shoulder surgery.

Q: Is it alright to tell me about the cameo part you had in the popular TV series 'Law and Order'?

Forrest Griffin: I got a bunch of crazy offers and that just seemed something like cool - and I liked 'Law and Order'. It's one of those shows which has been going on forever and you watch it growing up. I said "I'll do it", because I thought that would be cool. It was an easy part, something I can do without messing up too bad, so I did it. I played a fighter and a rapist with a small penis, so I think it was tailor made for me!

Q: When you battle with your opponents what goes through your dark mind?

Forrest Griffin: I'm not sure, I mean it's what I want to do and it's fun. It was super fun when I didn't care so much about results, when it wasn't my way of making a living, or the pressure of making a living where you want to send your kids to college. Now there's all that pressure but it's still fun to go out and try to beat the opponent and hit guys.

Q: You say mental preparation is unnecessary before you step into the octagon, is this true?

Forrest Griffin: It's not something that I do but I'm not saying its unnecessary. It's just not something which I've ever done. I try to develop a game plan and try to work on my game plan.

Q: Do you have any heroes?

Forrest Griffin: Yes, a guy named Patrick Telligman; he's one of my heroes. He played pro football in the NFL and he actually quit playing football to become an Honorary Ranger and he was killed in Iraq. He turned down $3 million-a-year for 30,000 dollars to go and be a hero. So I've always thought of him as a hero.

Q: What was it like promoting the UFC on the road?

Forrest Griffin: Doing different interviews, I don't do much of it and I'm not a real good traveler, what I want to do is fight people and what I like to do is stay home and train.

Q: Is it true you knocked out Kimbo Slice in a sparring match?

Forrest Griffin: I didn't actually, that's just one of those sparring stories that just kind of got a life of its own. I've heard that story before, but it never happened. I did spar with him but never knocked him out. Before I met him, I thought he was kind of a lark and I really didn't really respect him as a fighter and an

233

athlete. But now that I've met him and trained with him, I know he does the same work outs as I do and he wants it, he's making the best out of it. You really can't hit a guy who's trying to make the best out of himself; he's 34 and still learning the ground, he's a pretty athletic guy. Once you meet him, I think you'd wish him the best, he's not a bad guy.

Q: How was the Rampage Jackson fight put on at the UFC 86?

Forrest Griffin: Dana and Lorenzo came in and offered me a shot at the title, and I did what every guy would do; I jumped at it. Not only did Rampage have a good record but he had fought the best of the best. He's good at a lot of things; he's a good wrestler and a better striker. It's kind of funny that you see the guy all the time when you're filming the TUF and you know you are going to fight him in a couple of months time. But, it is what it is. The biggest thing in the fight was that I wanted to move with my feet, may be if I can get him on his back or may be surprise him a little with my wrestling. I don't think the fight was that controversial.

I'm seeing a lot of good fighters at 205 pounds. I don't worry too much now that I have the belt, it doesn't really make a lot of sense by troubling yourself by worrying. Once you get the belt I think anybody will tell you now it becomes, 'I've got to win my next fight'. I've never done anything super impressive so I'm looking to get the next win.

Q: What kind of activities do you take part in to relax and get away from all this fighting business?

Forrest Griffin: I actually don't watch fighting after I have my last fight if I can help it. I just relax and I don't have any fighting stuff in my house. I watch a lot of movies and television, I read a fair amount. I get stressed out a lot, I don't know why, but I'm a very hyper guy. Sometimes I'm laid back at other times you get hyper about stuff. I think obviously the

UFC is making a lot of progress and they are doing the marketing and doing the work. You have to understand that I started fighting for the first time in 1999, when I saw the first UFC I really couldn't understand why everybody was still watching other sports. I've been a lifelong basketball and football fan and I still follow the play offs, but I felt this [MMA] is so much better than everything else. It just seems to be more natural sport than the traditional sport fighting; I couldn't understand why everybody didn't love it. The goal for me was to make more money in fighting than I could in my other job.

GEORGES ST PIERRE
'THE RUSH'

Georges St. Pierre, often referred to simply as 'GSP', is the most successful Canadian UFC fighter to date. He had a difficult childhood growing up, being the victim of bullies in school. Often kids went as so far as stealing his money and clothes. Determined to make a break with the past, Georges started training in the martial arts at a young age and dreamed of becoming a UFC champion, after seeing Royce Gracie in the first Ultimate Fighting Championship.

After great success in smaller MMA events, GSP made his entrance onto the big stage in January 2004 at UFC 46. Since then, he has had a string of victories over some of the best fighters in his division, which include Matt Hughes, Matt Scrra, BJ Penn and Sean Sherk. He is the current UFC welterweight champion and trains at 'Jacksons MMA' gym in Albuquerque, New Mexico. GSP is known for his high level of skills in the octagon and his down to earth attitude towards fighters and fans alike.

Q: What was it like growing up in a small rural town in Canada?

Georges St Pierre: I was born in Quebec in a little country side place. I had problems at school which is one of the reasons I started training in the martial arts. At school, it was pretty bad and I had a really tough time. But I learned martial arts to defend myself and get out of trouble, and it also taught me discipline. It was different living in a small place. I was lonely and by myself, I did not go to school in my own town because in a small town like ours, there was no school. So I had to go to a school in the big city nearby. I didn't have a lot of friends because I was an outsider and always by myself. So I had trouble making friends at school, that's how it was.

Q: So what kind of incidents did you get into where gang life was the norm?

Georges St Pierre: When I was young I had a hard time. I had a problem making friends because I had problems with older teenagers. Because of this, other kids would avoid being my friend otherwise they would be targeted too. A bunch of teenagers who were five years older than us were making problems with the other kids. There were a lot of incidents with me. One time I was coming out of school and there were three or four guys outside. I was walking with my friend and we heard noises behind us. We were going to take the bus, and I said to my friend, "They just spat on us." My friend, said, "No, they didn't."

I turned around and I said to my friend, "Let's go to them," and he said "No, no I don't want to go." My friend, was small and the gang members were bigger and tall. I said, "You know what, you're never going to get respect if you don't make yourself respected." I went alone after them and hit the first guy, then I got beat up pretty bad because there were four of them. Even though I got beat up, they respected me because I came back for them. When you think about it, you realise it was stupid things which kids did at that age. I went back to fight them because of the honour and to earn respect. I had a lot of anger and pride in me when I was growing up, I didn't want to tell nobody about my problems. I had pride and a big ego, so I wouldn't tell anyone because I thought they'd say I'm like a baby or a kid who cannot defend himself.

Q: You took up martial arts as a kid, were you influenced by anyone in particular?
Georges St Pierre: I was influenced by Jean Claude Van Damme. I can't do the splits though [laughs]. I saw 'Blood Sport' which inspired me. This was a great inspiration to me. I wanted to be a karate or martial arts champion when I was young, so this was one of my goal. I started doing Kyoshin Karate, but when I was a teenager, after my teacher died I came across something different; I saw my first UFC. Then I started training for mixed martial arts.

Q: You worked as a bouncer, what was the experience like working in a rather tough environment?
Georges St Pierre: Now my life is pretty easy, I'm a world champion, but it hasn't always been like this. There was a time in my life when I was studying in school and working three jobs at same time. I was bouncing in a night club, working in a floor roofing place and for a government programme for teenagers at school. At the night club I was working with guys who were very big and strong, most of them were using violence to take care of the problems, but I never did that. I always thought the best way to take care of the problem was talking, so that's what I did most of the time to sort out problems.

Q: Is it true that your dream was to become a UFC champion?
Georges St Pierre: When I first saw Royce Gracie fighting in the UFC I was still a teenager, my teacher had died and I was very sad, and didn't know what to do. I wanted to keep training

in the martial arts but I felt I didn't know where to go and I felt lonely and by myself. Then when I saw Royce Gracie win the Ultimate Fighting Championship, I right away knew that was what I wanted to do. I didn't know much about the sport and in Canada know body knew what jiu-jitsu was because it was brand new.

So I tried to take jiu-jitsu classes to learn to grapple. But nobody knew much about this art but it was a very effective martial art. Royce Gracie is a definite inspiration for me and the pioneer of the sport, and no matter what happens now, he's always going to be a champion for me in my heart. He's somebody I look up to as an athlete.

Q: You actually had your first MMA fight at the age of 16 beating a 25 year old. Is this true?
Georges St Pierre: I have always been very good with my feet because of my karate training, and when I was 16 I started to learn jiu-jitsu. So I didn't know much on the ground, but I was very strong so I could power out of a submission from my opponent. At the time the sport was illegal, it was a secret No Holds Barred competition with open hand strikes on the floor. I had four amateur fights and I won all of them. I was a teenager fighting adults; this is before I was fighting professionally.

Q: You have stated in the past that you thought you were going to die when you fought Thomas Denny in a TKO Promotion, is this true?
Georges St Pierre: This was the toughest fight of my career, I was sick when I fought him, I couldn't breath. I dominated the first round with ground and pound, when I was in my corner I told my corner men I didn't want to go back for the second round because I thought I was going to die. My corner men pushed me and I ended up beating my opponent.

Q: Finally you made your UFC debut at UFC 44, what did

it feel like to be fighting in the UFC?
Georges St Pierre: I was fighting in MMA matches in my own country, Canada and I was undefeated at the time. I remember when Pete Spratt beat Robbie Lawler in a UFC bout, he was very tough and in the top rankings. Pete came to Canada to fight me and I beat him with a rear naked choke. This brought me to the attention of the UFC people, so they called my manger to offer me a fight in the UFC. It was a dream come true, the moment I had been waiting for a long time. Just to step into the octagon for first time, it was like I had a heart attack, it was an amazing feeling.

Q: Your UFC fight record is impressive; you fought Matt Hughes a couple of times and won the welterweight title from him. What was the feeling of achieving this and what do you think of him?
Georges St Pierre: Matt Hughes is the best opponent I have fought; he is a very good fighter. When Matt Hughes trains hard and he's at his best, he's very hard. He is the best fighter I have fought. It was an indescribable experience and an amazing feeling, something I had been waiting for a long time. Matt Hughes is getting old but I think he can come back if he keeps training hard. We have a new generation coming up now who are better athletes, but I think he can still do it. I never really had problems with Matt Hughes he was just talking to hype up the fight, but nothing personal. Actually, if I see Matt Hughes on the street in a situation and he needs help, I'll probably be the first person to stop and help him.

Q: Tell me, what went wrong in the BJ Penn Pen fight?
Georges St Pierre: BJ put his finger in my eye, I don't think it was intentional, I think it was an accident. That's no problem, stuff like that happens sometimes in a fight, I should've got on my knees and taken a few minutes out because I couldn't see anything. But I didn't because I was too much into the fight,

and I learned from my mistake and next time I will know how to react from my experience.

The first round was the worst because I could not see, I had to close one eye, and when you fight with one eye you're not accurate, the exchange of blows was not accurate. He had two eyes and I was fighting with one. When I came back to my corner my corner men wiped my eye with water and, after that, the eye got a little better. I should be fighting him again soon, it's not scheduled yet but I think it's in January. There are a lot of people looking forward to this fight and I think we should do it. I can't wait. I'm pretty sure we are going to fight each other very soon. I can beat him.

Q: You fought Matt Serra at UFC 69 and lost your title to him, but you came back and beat him in the second fight. Do you think he got in a lucky punch when he beat you?
Georges St Pierre: There's no such thing as a lucky punch. I didn't fight well the first time I fought him. Matt Serra was a better fighter on the night. I made many mistakes and got beat by a better man on the night, and hopefully I got a chance and went onto revenge my loss and showed that I'm better than when I performed in the first fight, when I beat Matt the second time. I had many problems outside the ring at the time, but I have no excuse, I lost the first fight because Serra was better than me. I should have won that fight but I lost and made a mistake, I lost my equilibrium from a punch and I just couldn't come back up. I'm a human being and humans make mistakes.

Q: It seems MMA is big in Canada, just how popular is it up there?
Georges St Pierre: It wasn't really that big until the UFC came to Montreal, now it's huge! There are a lot of fans everywhere and people want to see another UFC coming in Canada as soon as possible.

Q: Any disappointments so far in your career that come to mind?
Georges St Pierre: My biggest disappointment was when I lost the fight to Matt Serra. Always, a loss is hard to take in, but sometimes you realise it could be a good thing. It makes you change your routine and makes you think about why you lost and makes you a better fighter.

Q: Do you feel it is important to switch on and off, do you turn into another person when you enter the cage?
Georges St Pierre: When I go into a fight I forget all about my problems outside of the octagon and leave all the distractions outside. I focus on only one thing, and that is to beat my opponent.

Q: Do you think UFC fighters are the toughest athletes in the world?
Georges St Pierre: Most of them are the best athletes in the world. What we do is a mixture of fighting, boxing, kickboxing, wrestling, jiu-jitsu and judo, so we have to be very athletic. I train twice a day, six days a week. I do sprints, conditioning, boxing, wrestling, Muay Thai, Brazilian Jiu-Jitsu and mixed martial arts, all mixed together. My main coach is Greg Jackson but I have different coaches in different disciplines.

Q: Why did Diego Sanchez leave the Jackson camp?
Georges St Pierre: He left because he has a daughter in California, that's what everybody told me. I don't think he left because I came over to Jackson's, may be it has a little bit to do with this but I think it's more because of his daughter. In the future, there's a possibility of fighting him. He's pretty good; it depends on his next fight and my next fight.

Q: What do you think of boxing as a sport?
Georges St Pierre: I don't think we're in competition with

boxing; I'm a big fan of boxing as well.

Q: You're a big movie buff, will we be seeing you making a transition into Hollywood just as Randy Couture did?
Georges St Pierre: I think it's a possibility but right now I'm focusing on fighting and not on doing movies. Maybe one day if I have time I will pursue that avenue.

Q: What are your plans for the future?
Georges St Pierre: I fought John Fitch recently. John Fitch has a lot of heart, he's like the terminator; he never gives up and always comes back. I was happy with my performance. I will continue to fight in the sport, but I'm not one of those guys who fights because he has no choice, I fight because I love it and because there's a lot of money too.

If I wanted to I could have done something else because I have a diploma. The morning I wake up and I'm not happy with my job, then I'm going to do something else. If I didn't fight in MMA I could have been a professional trainer. I would like to thank my fans and also Affliction for the support they've given me.

KEITH JARDINE
'THE DEAN OF MEAN'

Keith Jardine is one of the top contenders in the UFC light-heavyweight division. Currently training at Greg Jackson's famed MMA academy in Albuquerque, New Mexico, Jardine first came to the public's attention when he was cast as a heavyweight under coach, Rick Franklin in TUF 2 series. Judging from first appearances, Jardine may resemble a tough mean looking biker with his shaved head and goatee beard, but in reality he's a really humble, soft spoken and down to earth individual.

Before entering the octagon he held several jobs; from bounty hunting, coaching his local football team, to personal training. The highlight of his MMA career came when he defeated former light-heavyweight champion Chuck Liddell by split decision at UFC 76. The intimidating warrior was on the verge of becoming one of the contenders to challenge for the title until his lost to Wanderlei Silva at UFC 84. However, Jardine still has a potentially good future in the UFC and is preparing for his next fight.

Q: Please tell me how you got involved in MMA.
Keith Jardine: Basically, I was a football coach in college, I got a degree in sports science. I was interested in personal training and after college I got into personal training for a bit. I was living in a really small town in New Mexico where I coached football, and I met one of Greg Jackson's students and I trained with him for a month or so. Then I realised that I had to get up really early, as it was a two hour drive to Jackson's gym. After training with him twice I decided to move out here and pursue fighting over here.

Q: What attracted you to the UFC and why get into this dangerous sport?
Keith Jardine: I saw the early UFCs and the technique they were doing back then didn't seem that difficult to me. I always kind of wanted to be a fighter but never got a chance to box or anything like that. When I first saw the UFC I had a wrestling background and thought it was something I would be able to do.

Q: Before you became a professional fighter, you did a lot of different jobs, fire fighter, bounty hunter, personal trainer can you shed light on your experiences?
Keith Jardine: Fire fighting was one of the proudest jobs I had; basically it was just hanging out with my friends and camping with my friends. It was the best and the proudest job I had. Putting out fires and cutting down trees was of course part of the job. I was into fitness, exercise and nutrition and then when I started helping other people I saw that as a personal trainer you really affect people's lives for the better and see the change in people. Once you start improving your health physically it transcends into everything else in your life. Conditioning is number one, more important than anything in our sport, It doesn't matter how much technique you know, it doesn't matter how good your game plan is, if you don't have the endurance to keep you going, then it's all over real fast.

As for bounty hunting, one of my good friends who ran a company needed extra guys so I worked for him for a little bit, it was fun and I only did it for about two months because I was really getting into the fighting sport of MMA at the time so the schedule just wouldn't allow me to stake people out in weird hours and always be ready to go, this didn't work with my training schedule. It wasn't too bad as a job, most of the times when we went to pick somebody up they were waiting for you, sometimes it was a relief that they were finally picked up. A couple of times I had to run people down, but no big deal.

Q: Experiences on the TUF series?
Keith Jardine: A good friend of mine was on season one, he' s the one who helped me out to get on the season two. On the season two, actually behind the scenes they really did a lot of cool behind the scenes stuff. They made the fights three rounds and a lot of the fights went the distance. After the fights they had a few minutes to show everything else what went on, there were a lot of pranks that went on behind the scenes which not a lot of people know about, I think that's really too bad because this would have made the season a lot better.

To be on TUF is the best career choice I've ever made. It just gives you the incredible opportunity, after the show you're a full time professional fighter, you can fight and give up your day job. You can train two or three times a day and if you take advantage of the popularity it gives you, it really helps you become a top fighter.

When I had my first MMA fight I didn't really know what to think, or what to expect, it was kind of getting into a real fight, like a street fight. I was really pumped up and the adrenaline was high and I felt like I was walking into a bar and getting into a fight, you get in the cage the door locks and there's no going back. After that you get more professional about it, but at first it felt like I was getting in to a real fight.

Q: Can anyone off the street become a MMA fighter?

Keith Jardine: It's hard, I've had pro boxing fights before but the MMA fights are very hard. I think the training in boxing is kind of easy because all you have got to do is box, hit mitts and get in shape. But as MMA fighters, we have to train everything, with world class wrestlers, world class jiu-jitsu guys, world class boxers and find a way to bring everything together and make it flow together, which is so hard to do. You can't forget one thing whilst concentrating on the other, there's true science to MMA training for sure.

I could play basketball and go shoot baskets and I actually got good at it one time too, but that doesn't mean I'm going to be able to go in the NBA and play with any of those professional guys, I'd get creamed. Fighting is the same way. Anyone can pick up a basketball and someone on the street thinks he's pretty good but he's not going to be able to play in the NBA.

Q: Am I right in saying most of your wins have come from knock outs?

Keith Jardine: It's more fun to knock out the opponent, my background is actually in jiu-jitsu, I won a lot of national grappling tournaments. That was something I was known for a long time and what I'm best at, but I have fun fighting and throwing punches and kicks most of my fights usually end up in a knock out. For me, technique comes last because if you take anybody you can teach anybody technique if you have time, but the most important thing is you have to have the heart and the right spirit to get into the sport. If your spirit isn't strong then you're going to get tested, so your spirit is first and the number one. Then you have to have the proper training and fitness so you can execute all the techniques which is also important, of course.

Q: Do you think some people have a misconception of what

a fighter really looks and acts like ?
Keith Jardine: For me most of the top level fighters are nice and humble people, because we get our aggression out in the ring, there's no reason to walk around with a chip on our shoulders. We're all professionals and very happy to have what we have so all the top level fighter are great guys.

Q: You fought Forrest Griffin, is it true he actually underestimated you?
Keith Jardine: No, I guarantee you he didn't underestimate me, it was just my night that day.

Q: Were you surprised that you got a shot at Chuck Liddell?
Keith Jardine: First I didn't believe it - I was going to fight Chuck Liddell and I was extremely excited; that's why I'm here for and that is to measure myself against the best in the world. He happened to be one of the all time best so I didn't hesitate at all in the fight, it's a fight I definitely wanted. My game plan in that fight was to do what I do well, throwing good combinations, kicks and the main thing was keeping focused. My focus for that fight was to maintain my focus because, with Chuck, if you blink at the wrong time or turn your head the wrong time he's going to you knock you out. I was very confident and I fully expected to win that fight. What did surprise me was it went to a decision and I still got the win because the judges sometimes like the big stars, I was kind of worried when it went to decision but I wasn't surprised at all, just very tired.

Q: Will there be 'Keith Jardine versus Chuck Liddell II'?
Keith Jardine: Yes, I'm sure it will happen, I'll fight Forrest again and Chuck again too. If my career is strong enough it will happen.

Q: Do you have to switch on and off mentality?

Keith Jradine: You have to have that, you can't be 'on' all the time you can't think about fighting all the time because it'll just wear you out. That's why I'm hesitant to do too many interviews in my time off, you need to have that separation. On the subject of keeping a clear mind when fighting, I think when you have fought so many times you gain experience, you learn through training to keep calm and - in the cage - if you don't, you're going to get tired and make bad mistakes. When GSP fought Fitch more recently it was a 5-round fight, there were ups and downs, but he was incredibly calm all the way through. That's the way it's supposed to be like.

Q: When you fought Wanderlei Silva do you think if you had beaten him you would be fighting for the title right now?
Keith Jardine: I felt great before the fight and everything was just fine, I knew he was awkward   and he threw heavy punches from weird angles that's what caught on real quickly. He timed my leg kicks and used his hands well, it's pretty hard to recover from that. I would be fighting for the title right now, but that's OK because I'm going to have a long career. After a defeat, you just check out what you did wrong and if there's anything to learn from it and get back to work and that's what I do. I fought a really good opponent so there's not much point to feel bad about it, because I can erase that loss really quick.

Q:What are your long term goals in the UFC ?
Keith Jardine: I'm   going to be here for a long time and the UFC loves the way I fight, I'm not too flashy but all my fights are really exciting, I'm going to be here for a long time.

Q: What is it for you which makes MMA so exciting?
Keith Jardine: I think there's a lot of reasons that makes MMA really exciting. First of all in boxing, some people don't have enough attention to watch 10 or 12 rounds. In the UFC you

really build up the characters and the people really have interest in the characters, so it's more entertainment for the fans that way too. It makes the sport more exciting. When you watch fighting you want to watch the best fighting in the world and MMA fighters are the best and most exciting to watch. Combat sports are the essence of all competition. Put one guy against another guy, there's no excuses or team to fall behind. The better guy's going to win and everybody can relate to that.

Q: Any particular fighter you would have liked to fight or would like to fight in the near future?
Keith Jardine: Right now, the guy I want to fight is Brandon Vera, the way he fights, he's a stand up guy with punches and kicks which is my kind of fighting I can't ask for much more. He's the guy I want for sure.

Q: Finally, What do you think of the architect behind the redevelopment of UFC organisation, Dana White? Do you think the UFC and the sport of MMA will continue its meteoric rise or come to a stand-still?
Keith Jardine: Dana White is great because I wouldn't be where I am today without him. He's turned the sport into what it is today and deserves a lot more credit than he gets for that. The sport was dying and now they're making a lot of money and I'm making a little bit of money too and, in the future, I hope I'm making more money.

Dana is just fine with me for sure. I have developed my own clothing line called 'Meanstyle', which I put a lot of input into. I'm pretty excited about it. The sky is the limit; we have old fighters like Chick Liddell and all the established fighter s who make the sport what it is today. Then you've got new guys coming up and once they get to the top things will get bigger and better and really explode. It's exciting with the UFC going all over the world; I heard it's going to go to places like Dubai which is just incredible.

ANDERSON SILVA
'THE SPIDER'

Over his years of professional MMA competition, Anderson 'The Spider' Silva has held each of the UFC, Cage Rage and Shooto Middleweight championship belts. Born and bred in Brazil, Silva was a member of the famous Chute Boxe Academy at the height of its infamy.

Like many of the UFC stars of today, Silva fought in a number of organisations such as the Pride Fighting Championships and Cage Rage, before going on to conquer the UFC. He has been described by many as, pound for pound, the best fighter in the world. Known for his devastating knock outs and equally potent Brazilian Jiu-Jitsu skills, he has been a dominating force in the UFC and the Muay Thai practitioner has clearly proven his position as the Number 1 middleweight fighter in the world.

He made his light-heavyweight debut against James Irvin in July 2008 and barely broke a sweat as he smashed the American within the first round. Silva is part of the 'Black House' team and runs an academy with fellow member Antonio Nogueira in Florida and continues to impress us with his winning streak.

Q: Can you tell me of your experiences fighting in Japan and what made you go to fight there?
Anderson Silva: My experiences in Japan were really good and this gave me the basis and experience to fight in other events. For me, going to fight in Japan was the natural course of my career.

Q: Which was your hardest fight in Japan?
Anderson Silva: Basically, all of my fights were pretty tough, but my toughest fight was in Shooto against Sakurai, when I won the belt. Sakurai had beaten many Brazilians and had no losses in Shooto, but I was very prepared for the fight with a strong team behind me. My goal was to win that fight; it was tough, but I did my job right and accomplished my goal.

Q: You also fought in Cage Rage and became the champion. How did you find the experience fighting in Europe?
Anderson Silva: Fighting in Cage Rage was good. I had my good and bad moments but in the end they promoted me very well. I also got used to fighting in the cage and it gave people a chance to know me a little better and eventually lead my entry into the UFC.

Q: How did you get involved with the UFC? Was this your ultimate goal?
Anderson Silva: It was a big dream of mine to fight in the UFC and it was a natural course of things where you evolve and end up pursuing your dream when you train hard and do your job well. I was always a big fan of the UFC.

Q: You demonstrated awesome skills at UFC 64 fight against Rich Franklin, can you shed some light on this ground breaking fight?
Anderson Silva: I felt good going into the fight and for the belt and it was an honour to fight Rich Franklin. I respect him for

giving me the opportunity. I was very prepared for this fight. I was very well trained for this fight and the goal was to fight for the title. I trained really hard for this the whole way, and it's what happens when you're given a chance and you come prepared. You carry out your game plan you have been training for. It's my job.

Q: You demolished Franklin for the second time at UFC 77 with 20 consecutive knees. Do you think this proved you had the potential to 'clean up' your division?
Anderson Silva: I trained even harder for the second fight with Rich Franklin because I knew he was in very good shape and he had trained very hard for this fight. I was doing my job. Rich had a very bad moment when he made a mistake and I got him. The sport has evolved now to a point what it is now and people want to see a good fight and usually a good fight involves good stand up knock outs. My goal is to go in and do my job, it would be great if the both of us walked out uninjured, but that's not always possible.

Q: Do you ever feel pressure, as you are undefeated so far in the UFC?
Anderson Silva: No, not at all, it's just a natural course of things. I just have to do my job well and show up to the fight, and forget about that I own the belt.

Q: What motivates you to fight in such a dangerous sport?
Anderson Silva: I fight because it's satisfying, and I know I can do a good job and go out there showing I'm one of the best. I've been training all my life, it's very natural for me.

Q: Who inspired you in MMA and what did you do to make a living before becoming a professional fighter?
Anderson Silva: I didn't plan or even think of becoming a professional fighter but I would always watch Carlson Gracie,

Royce Gracie, Marco Ruas and Vitor Belfort fight. So I had some Brazilian fighting idols but I didn't make that my lifelong dream, but things just happened naturally. I've always had to work; I've been an office assistant, worked in McDonalds for six years but I always found a way to train and have been linked to the martial arts. I've been a professional fighter for a long time now but really now the UFC has expanded and it's something completely different because the sport is huge in the media now, so it's a completely different setting for me.

Q: Did you ever get into any street fights in Brazil as it is quite common there?
Anderson Silva: I've never had that problem in Brazil, MMA is a sport and street fighting is not. People have to know how to differentiate between the two.

Q: Can you tell me in your fight against Okami at the 'Rumble on the Rock' promotion why you got disqualified?
Anderson Silva: No comment.

Q: How do you prepare for a fight?
Anderson Silva: You have to be very focused the whole way through even when you are not training for a fight. If you get your head in place and train you will always be prepared. I'm very focused and concentrating 100% before the fight and that's my job to go out there and do my best. After the fight I try to get my mind off things and just relax.

Q: Michael Bisping has stated in past he would like to fight you; what do you think of him?
Anderson Silva: He's a great fighter and he's starting to build himself up and he could be a good challenge in the future. I can't say that I would like to fight him; I want to fight the best, so if he is one of the best, who knows, one day. Michael Bisping is a great fighter but I cannot predict the fight because you'll

just have to see it if the time comes.

Q: Why are you a big fan of Spider Man?

Anderson Silva: I relate to Spiderman and have always done so because I think he's a super hero who's got bills to pay, so I could always relate to him and how he also has to struggle.

Q: Were you ever influenced by Bruce Lee?

Anderson Silva: I've always been a big fan and watched all of his movies. He was my idol, even Brandon Lee. I looked up to both of them.

Q: You expressed your desire to fight top professional boxer Roy Jones Junior - would you definitely like to face him in the future?

Anderson Silva: Boxing and MMA are two completely different things, but MMA has its great champions as well as boxing. MMA might be in the spotlight right now because of what the UFC has done for the sport. Boxing has got to be respected because they have some great champions. I've always wanted to fight a great boxer, it's my dream to fight Roy Jones and I hope in the near future this fight will happen. The sport of MMA is growing very fast and new athletes are going to come on board and if they [boxers] think they can make that decision, then they probably will most likely go into MMA.

Q: How did you prepare for the James Irvin fight?

Anderson Silva: My training is always the same no matter who my opponent is. I did the same training with a few adjustments here and there for this fight such as a wearing a weight jacket when I was training.

Q: You have planted a seed in America by opening a state of the art MMA gym in Miami, how is that venture doing?

Anderson Silva: The gym is going well, we have a professor

there in charge, we are doing this to educate people in MMA and trying to get the focus on the sport. Obviously MMA in the U.S. is more in the media spotlight right now and even though we've been doing it for a long time in Brazil, where it's got its heritage and is a traditional sport, it's not so much in the headlines compared to America. But it's getting more and more attention now and people are respecting it now. It can get even bigger and that's what they're working hard at and there are chances it will.

Q: Do you plan on 'cleaning out' the light-heavyweight division which will make you an all time great UFC fighter?
Anderson Silva: I'm trained to fight the best; whoever the UFC puts in front of me, I'll fight. I have no plans to stay in the 205lb division; my place is at 185 defending my title, leaving the 205 title to Lyoto [Machida].

Q: How many more years do you plan on fighting and do you have other goals you would like to focus on after retiring?
Anderson Silva: I have maybe another two or three years, who knows. But my dream after fighting in MMA is everyone knows me by now. My proudest moment has been my first title defence because it was a tough thing to do and I defended it successfully. It's hard to go undefeated, but that's what I'm training for. My life is moving slowly and I just have to keep training hard and fighting in the UFC and reach my goals. Other than that I have to leave it in the hands of God and keep doing my job. I want to thank my fans and all of my trainers and anyone who's a part of my team

MICHAEL BISPING

'THE COUNT'

Michael 'The Count' Bisping is no doubt the most famous and successful British fighter to compete in the UFC to date. This charismatic former-DJ is a fan favourite. Born in Cyprus, Bisping moved to North West of England as a child and started training in martial arts. He has held a number of domestic MMA titles including the Cage Rage and FX3 light-heavyweight championships.

Bisping came to the attention of a wider audience after he won the TUF 3 series which aired early 2006. After securing a contract with the UFC, he kept hold of unbeaten record until his only loss to date to Rashad Evans, at UFC 78. One of the most enthusiastic UFC fighters and the organisation's poster boy for the UK, Bisping continues to enjoy fighting in a sport he loves. He admits he is 'living the dream'. Many observers feel he is destined to make history by becoming the first ever UFC champion from the UK.

259

Q: Can you please shed some light on your childhood upbringing?
Michael Bisping: I was born in Cyprus, on an army base, as my dad was in the military. We spent a couple of years there and then moved to Clitheroe, in the North West of England. We moved a little bit, to various houses as you do when you're in the army, but I can't really remember too much about that. Then we settled back in Clitheroe where I've spent most of my life. I had a pretty much normal upbringing, my parents never had too much money but they always tried to give us the best things they could.

I got involved in the martial arts at the age of 9. I always enjoyed martial arts movies and any movies with fights such as Rocky films and the old 80's Ninja movies, Jean Claude Van Damme and Bruce Lee movies. My brother started to go to jiu-jitsu classes and I wanted to tag along and went from there and fell in love with it. I went to school around here, I enjoyed school and did quite well in the class but I never tried or put too much effort into my school work; that was my problem. I got fairly decent grades but could have done better. It always said in school reports, "Michael could do a lot better if he tried harder". I suppose I could have done better but I was too busy training martial arts and messing around, trying to be the class clown.

Q: Is it true you were banned from soccer because of your dirty tackles?
Michael Bisping: I was quite rough on the football pitch; I did a lot of shoulder barges so it used to make people mad. I started playing rugby because it suited me a lot more, I played for the Clitheroe youth team and moved on to the Blackburn team. I was pretty decent at football I and was a bit bigger than the other kids. I was very competitive and always have been. I used to go for the ball, and if I didn't get it I would keep trying.

Q: When you started competing in martial arts did you feel the need to go out and get a proper job in order to make a living?

Michael Bisping: When I was younger I used to go to a lot of amateur tournaments and the kickboxing. I used to get paid for the fights but it wasn't much, I think £250, something like that. So you can't really make a living out of that, and to be honest, at the time I didn't really look at martial arts as a way of making a living and a profession, it was more as a hobby and a way to keep fit. It was something I enjoyed and like many people, did it for the passion of it.

I met my girlfriend and had a couple of kids and I had a couple of kick boxing fights before I met her. Then, this was not really something I would make a living from so I kind of gave up on it. We had kids and I went onto hold down a full time job and looking after the kids. This didn't leave me much time for training but I had done it all ever since I was a kid, so I suppose I wasn't bored with it but had done it for a long time, and I was working various jobs.

At the age of 22 I thought to myself, "What am I doing with myself? Where's my life going?" Like I said, I always did pretty well in school and considered myself intelligent but I was working some jobs which didn't really require any qualifications or any real intelligence. I thought I could be doing something more useful in this world, so I used to think, "What I could be doing?"

To be honest, I toyed around with the idea of going back to university. I used to do DJ'ing on the side on the weekends. So I thought I'd DJ on the weekend and go to university during the week and try to get decent qualifications or a degree, which is something that would get me a better job and provide a better home and more income for my family, just to generally better myself because I wasn't happy with the way I turned out.

The more I thought about it, the more I kept coming back to the martial arts. Then I thought to myself, "I've always been good at this", so I thought I'd try to be a boxer. Mixed martial arts was around, but it wasn't really big as we see it today, and I didn't know too much about MMA to be honest. So I started to be a boxer and trained in the boxing gym and had a couple of fights and won them all by TKO.

I got in touch with my old jiu-jitsu instructor from years ago who was in Nottingham, and he told me about mixed martial arts and that I'd be really good at it. I was doing some competitions as a kid but I didn't know at the time but it was actually amateur mixed martial arts. A couple of guys I beat quite easily had gone onto fight in the UFC and have fairly decent careers. So this is something I started to think about. I gave up work and started training for mixed martial arts.

Q: How did you get onto the TUF series?
Michael Bisping: I started training for mixed martial arts and I was doing really well in the U.K, I won all my fights. Any belt in the UK on offer, I'd won. I also held the British kickboxing title at the time. So I started thinking about looking overseas and fighting in larger promotions, ultimately the UFC which was where I wanted to be.

My manager, Anthony at the Wolfslair gym contacted the UFC and gave me a contract in the UFC, they said they'd had their eye on me and would give me a fight in the UFC with no problem. But they thought I'd be great for 'The Ultimate Fighter.' They said they had an upcoming season of TUF which would feature light-heavyweights and middleweights and they were looking for an English guy. They told me they were going to have auditions in London and asked if I could attend the auditions.

In the mean time, I spoke to the executives at Spike TV who were creating the show, I was pretty much chosen before I went to the auditions. I'd already beaten the other light-heavyweights who attended the auditions, so this made me the obvious choice really. So I went to the audition and the process.

I was told I was on the show and to keep it quiet. The next day they flew eight of us English guys out to Vegas. While we were there we were locked in a hotel room for a week and weren't allowed to leave at all. The reason being is they didn't want us bumping into each other, there were fighters from America all over the place who were trying out for the show, and didn't want people to know who was on and leaking details, it was all to do with confidentiality.

It was horrible, to say the least, to be stuck in a hotel room. They brought us three meals a day and the meals weren't very nice. If we walked out from the room and got caught we would have blown our chance of getting on the show. So it was a case of sitting in the room and reading a book or watching the same movies over and over again. I got called into the interview room, I was there for a few minutes and cracked a silly joke, everybody in the room laughed their heads off and they said "Yes, you will be perfect for it, get out of here, you need to just pass your medical test and we'll get you on the show!"

Behind the scenes, there were quite a lot of stuff and heated arguments that went on when filming between the fighters, which I thought would have made it onto the show. But I suppose it had to relate to the story line so they left them out. There were various different film crews walking around the house the whole time, they had cameras in the corners of the rooms as well but actual crews and sound guys. Every time, let's say someone's upstairs in a different room and you're sat in the kitchen, a feud starts upstairs and the crew go rushing upstairs as the production team would tell them someone's talking shit upstairs. We weren't allowed to speak to the film crew at all, if we spoke to them we could lose our job. When we all got bored we would try to get the film crew to talk to us but they wouldn't respond.

Q: When you won the series did you feel you had actually 'arrived' at UFC?

Michal Bisping: Yes absolutely, it was weird. When Anthony from the Wolfslair gym had got in touch with the UFC, he mentioned TUF to me, and said, "You're going to go in there and you're going to win it." That was obviously the plan. I was going to go in there and try to win it, having aspirations to win the thing and actually winning it are completely two different things. But that's what I went in there to do; and that was to win. That was my mind set. I wasn't going out there to make friends, but to win at any cost.

Every time I won a fight I was very pleased and was getting just that close to it, one more fight and I'm in the final. The guy I was fighting was Josh Haynes; I was comfortable as I knew I could beat him so I was excited about that. When I won the fight by TKO, I just collapsed on the floor, star-shaped with my arms and legs out. It was just a sheer relieve, the pressure I had put on myself and pressure to win and provide for my family, everything I had done to that point, the sacrifice in choosing this career finally it paid off.

I won a decent contract in the UFC which meant my family was going to have a little bit of more money. So, I collapsed on the floor and the doctor comes up to me and says, "Are you OK?"I said, "Yes, I'm fine there's nothing wrong with me. I'm just lying on the floor, it's a sheer relief." It was a great moment.

Q: You were stripped off the Cage Rage belt, why was that?
Michael Bisping: I'm not sure, to be honest. I fought in Cage Rage in my third pro fight and I was supposed to fight [Renato] Babalu [Sobral], but he didn't fight because he was injured or something. So I fought Mark Epstein who was their champion and was the co- promoter's friend. I think they brought me in just to get beat up, they never expected me to go in there and win, thinking Mark Epstein would destroy me.

Anyway, I went in there and I beat him by TKO in the second round. They said Mark didn't have enough time to prepare and he wasn't ready, so they set up a rematch instantly. I said, "Yes, no problem, I'll fight him again." So I fought again and this time I won by a knockout in the third round. I thought it was pretty clear that I beat him fair and square both times. I had a couple of fights with other organisations. Later I found out I'd been stripped of my title when I read it on the internet to be honest.

I was going through the Cage Warriors forums and came across the news 'Michael Bisping stripped off his Cage Rage title'. So I looked at the Cage Rage website and it had the same thing on there too. So I rang up Andy Geer [co- promoter] and asked him, "What's going on here?" He said, "Yes, we've had no choice but to strip you." I asked him why and he said it was because of management issues. "What do you mean management issues?" I asked. He said, "We can't really go into it". I told him, "I don't know what you're talking about; so is that it, I'm stripped of my title just like that?" He said, "I'm really sorry Michael", and he put the phone down on me. That was my feud with Cage Rage.

To be honest, I think they didn't want me to be the champion in the first place, they were trying to build up their own guy and wanted someone from London to have the belt, so they can sell more tickets. Every time I fought in Cage Rage I've always brought coach loads of people with me. I suppose they wanted someone from London to be the champion, I'm not sure. I fought in Cage Warriors and they were great and looked after me. I fought for them a number of times and this was a good organization to work for.

Q: You're the 'Ricky Hatton' of MMA in the UK, how are you treated by the fans?
Michael Bisping: The fans are amazing; it blows my mind to see I've got fans. Doesn't seem quite right with me as I feel I'm just a normal guy. A few years ago, I wouldn't even have dreamt about having this conversation. To say I've got fans,

seems a bit strange and alien to me, I suppose. I'm fighting in front of big crowds and TV. They're amazing wherever I meet them. They just want to meet me, or want a picture or an autograph and have nice things to say. I always get kind messages through my website whether it's England, America or Canada.

I remember when I fought in Canada, I was walking in Montreal and a huge crowd gathered, I must have been there for three hours. If people are standing in a line or in a crowd to see me or shake my hand I won't just walk off and say I've got to go, because these people are waiting. I remember in Montreal it was a huge crowd, 350 people all gathered around and I was there for about two hours taking pictures. It was very surreal. I was with a couple of my friends and we were laughing our heads off, having a good time. They'd never seen anything like it. The fans are amazing and I feel blessed and very fortunate.

Q: Your only loss came to Rashad Evans, do you feel you would have won had there been no point system?
Michael Bisping: Absolutely, if the fight was a 5-round fight or there was no point system - where you carry on until someone wins - I would have definitely won the fight. At the end of the fight, Rashad was out of gas but I was fine. He won the first round I won the second, the third was very close. I think end of the third round he was tired, he got me down - it wasn't really a takedown but more of a scramble - and he ended up on the top. I think that's what clinched the fight for Rashad, that's why he was awarded the fight.

Two judges said he won, one judge said I'd won. Looking back in hindsight, I should have pushed the pace a little more, he was tired and I was fresh. Rashad is a tough character, he's undefeated, there's no shame in it and I learned a lot from that fight.

Q: Charles McCarthy fired verbal assaults your way before

the fight, how did you react to this?
Michael Bisping : He was very critical about my abilities; my entire game. Before the fight I'd done a few interviews about Charles McCarthy and I said in my interviews that I'd never met the guy and that I had nothing against him. I had no opinion of the guy. He was an average guy and may the best man win. But he went on to do interviews with the British press, I'm not sure if he was trying to play mind games but he went onto say, basically, I had no skills, I was the most average fighter in the UFC, and that I didn't have any ground game, wrestling and no striking and there was nothing I could really do to him.

I was pretty pissed off by that to be honest, it was very insulting. It was in the British press so a lot of people were reading about all this. So I thought I want to make an example of this guy and I feel I did that in the fight. I completely dominated the guy, I hit him with every combination under the sun, and hit him 25 knees effectively and dropped him in the first round, he could never continue.

Q: Regarding your relationship with mainstream media, have you got any interesting stories about your contact with them?
Michael Bisping: On the whole, now compared to couple of years ago the media have taken more interest in covering the sport and more people are interested in the sport. The media can't deny the fact that the sport is growing and people want to know about it. Maybe, at the start, that wasn't the case, but they are very welcoming towards it now. They ask intelligent questions about the sport, as opposed to the start - where they asked stupid questions like "Is it dangerous?" or "Has anyone died yet?"

Now the reporters know what they're talking about. Controversial stories? I remember in the lead up to the UFC 70 at Manchester, in the M.E.N. arena. I had a radio interview with BBC Manchester, a lady who presents the weather sometimes -

blonde hair in her mid-forties, can't remember her name. Anyway, I go in and sat in the studio and she's talking on air and I'm waiting sitting there. She says on air, "Up next, if you've ever seen the film 'Fight Club', our next guest is Michael Bisping, who fights in the UFC."

So then she turns to me she says, "Right Michael, so you fight in the UFC", and I said, "Yes". She says, "Look at the size of you, how big are you? You must be at least 18 stone?"

I'm about 14 stone, I'm not a small guy but I'm not overly big. And she says, "You're 18 stone and covered in scars." I said, "I'm not covered in scars, I've got a few scars on my head, I banged my head as a kid but I'm not covered in scars."

She says, "This sport is for thugs isn't it?"

I said, "No, it's not for thugs."

She says, "It's barbarians!"

I said, "It's not a sport for barbarians…"

She says, "Well, you look like a barbarian."

And, I said, "Really? I'll keep my thoughts on what you look like to myself shall I?" She looked like mutton dressed as lamb. Then she started criticising the sport saying people can die. I said to her, "Well, have you ever watched sport?"

She said, "No."

I said, "How the hell can you sit there passing judgment and talking about the sport when you've never even seen it? What are you basing these facts on anyway ?" We got into an argument on air; basically, she didn't have a leg to stand on. She wrapped the interview and ushered me out.

After the UFC 70, I went back to the hotel and we were celebrating , there was me, my girlfriend and a few of my close friends. We were sat at a table with Randy Couture, Jean Claude Van Damme and Wayne Rooney; it was quite surreal. I was always a fan of Van Damme when I was a kid. I was in a good mood and having a few drinks and a good laugh.

Q: What do you think of Royce Gracie, the pioneer of MMA?

Michael Bisping: Royce Gracie, just like you said, is a pioneer of the sport and the Gracie family in general did great things for the sport. They came up with idea of the UFC. He won the early UFC's a couple of times and he's a great fighter and a legend in the sport.

Q: Your friend, the heavyweight boxer, David Haye has taken interest in MMA. Do you think he maycompete in the future?

Michael Bisping: We're quite friendly and he's a great guy, he's a fantastic great boxer and a credit to British boxing. Yes, I've read interviews where he's said himself he's planning to get into MMA eventually, after he's done with boxing. I think David Haye, in boxing, will really shake up the heavyweight division and he's definitely got what it takes I think to be a UFC champion.

He's like a world class boxer with heavy hands, he already knows a bit about the wrestling and jiu-jitsu. The kind of determination and the fighting spirit he already has, combined that with Brazilian Jiu-Jitsu and wrestling and stand up MMA game which he already has been expanding on a little bit; yes, he's got potential to do great things in the sport. I mean he's already doing great things in thc world of boxing, a world champion and probably the best British boxer at the moment. If the guy came into MMA then I'd say, "Watch out, all the heavyweights!"

Q: Do you feel boxers had lot more respect before than martial arts fighters until the UFC changed things?

Michael Bisping: Yes, I suppose I can understand what you're saying. Boxing has always been televised in households all across the country; people worldwide always have had respect for boxers. It's big money and boxers are recognised as athletes.

It wasn't always the case with martial arts, it is something you did as a hobby or to keep fit. I don't think martial artists were ever classed as athletes or even respected for their fighting ability.

Now the UFC, not just the UFC which is the most dominant that everyone knows about, but MMA has made a transition into the mainstream now. Since this happened, people realise martial artists should be taken seriously and the skills you learn whether its Thai boxing or, Brazilian Jiu-Jitsu are good, and these men have got serious fighting ability. It's definitely a good thing.

Q: Who are your favourite UFC fighters?
Michael Bisping: Right now I've got to say I love watching Anderson Silva fight. The guy's a great fighter and great to watch. He's a very dominant champion; he's got a very good style which I like to watch. Roger Huerta is good to watch, lots of things about the UFC is they've got some great fighters. I tend to watch more strikers than a wrestler who just want to take someone down and control his opponent.

I admire the skill involved and good jiu-jitsu. I love to watch great jiu-jitsu, but if someone takes someone down and lie on top of the opponent, and win with points decision, I'm not really a fan of that. I like to watch a bit of action. Not everyone gets along in this world; on the whole most of the fighters in the UFC, as a matter of fact in MMA in general, are decent guys. Me and Matt Hamill - who was on TUF with me - didn't get on too well, but we've kind of buried the hatched on that. We had a little fall out, its old news now, you don't hold grudges.

Q: Anderson Silva seems to be dominating everyone he fights; do you think you can beat him?
Michael Bisping: I hope to fight Anderson Silva. Number one is; you have to earn the right to fight some on like Anderson Silva, he's the best in the world. You've got to earn the right

which is what I'm doing right now by building myself up; working my way up to get that privilege to fight him. He's probably pound-for-pound the best fighter in the world, so if I get that chance, I'll take that fight seriously. This is definitely what I want to do and achieve.

No one's really been able to test him yet, so I would like to go in there and see what I can do. I think I could test him and definitely give him a good fight. We'll have to wait and see. A lot of people think when someone goes in there up against him he just wipes them out and destroys them. I'm training really hard now, I'm not still the finished product, there's a lot of areas I want to get better at. I'm happy with my progress that I've made.

After the next fight I'm taking a trip out to Thailand again, training Thai boxing, then I'm off to Brazil to work on my jiu-jitsu. I'm willing to make the sacrifices that I've got to make to be the best I can. Hopefully when I get the chance I'll take the advantage and beat him.

Q: How is your relationship with Dana White?
Michael Bisping: lot of people talk a lot of shit on the internet about him but they don't know what they're talking about. Dana White takes good care of fighters; he really looks after me and looks after all the fighters. He always says, "If you need any advice or anything, call me at 1 in the morning, anytime, and I'll be there for you." And he sticks to his word. He takes care of us, he helps us out financially; the UFC is like a big family. I haven't got a bad word to say about Dana to be honest.

Q: What would you be doing today to make a living if you did not turn to professional fighting in the UFC?
Michael Bisping: I don't know; I'm not sure. I did put a lot of effort being a DJ when I was younger which I enjoyed, but felt it wasn't a proper job and I wasn't going to be big; only a few people in the world have achieved that. I always enjoyed

construction work, enjoyed building things so may be something along these lines. This was my problem as a kid, when I left school I didn't know what I wanted to do. I was very envious of those who knew exactly what they wanted to pursue... I never did. That is why I didn't end up going to university because I didn't know what course I wanted to do.

To answer your question, I wouldn't know. When I was a kid I was a big fan of Frank Bruno, to me he was a great boxer and a great character. The future for me is just keep on training and keep fighting in the UFC and may be when I get towards the end of my fighting career I'd want to open my own academy and train fighters, or may be manage fighters when I'm done. I've got a lot of experience and I know a lot about the business now that I can offer the upcoming fighters.

The UFC has changed my life utterly and completely. I'm still the same person and I always will be. I've got more money now, that's the main difference - we could afford the nice things in life. On the whole, the main thing on how it's changed my life is I was never happy doing the other jobs I did, I used to hate them to be honest. Now I'm earning more money, but the main thing is I'm doing something I love, I'm very lucky.

I love training and I love working out, so I'm fortunate I'm able to make a living in what I love to do. I'm really passionate about my job which reflects on my whole life. I'm not angry; I'm a happy person on the whole. So, me and my family are happy. I want to thank all the fans from the bottom of my heart for all the support I get from everyone; it truly amazes me every time. Whenever I walk out to fight in England the crowd go crazy, they're very excited and passionate, it blows my mind. Thanks for all the support and I hope I continue to entertain you with my fights.

SEAN SHERK
'MUSCLE SHARK'

Alife-long competitor, 'The Muscle Shark' began
wrestling at the age of 7 and started training in
MMA at the 'Minnesota Martial Arts Academy'
way back in 1994 with the famed coach and BJJ black belt,
Greg Nelson. Sherk is an advocate of hard training and has
put together a rigorous regime with the help of some
innovative strength and conditioning coaches, who have
come up with some influential new methods to ensure that
Sherk is in the best physical condition possible.

Like many UFC fighters, Sherk fought in some smaller
MMA shows before fighting in the UFC. Some of the top names
he's fought in the UFC include Matt Hughes, BJ Penn and
Georges St Pierre. Sean Sherk became the UFC lightweight
champion on October 14 2006 when he beat Kenny Florian at
UFC 64, however, Sherk's dream soon turned into a nightmare
as he was stripped of the title after testing positive for steroids.
However, he continues to compete and vehemently denies
accusations that he has used performance-enhancing drugs.

Q: What is your martial arts background and who influenced you as a martial artist in the early days of your training?

Sean Sherk: When I was young I started wrestling at the age of 7. I wrestled competitively for 13 years and I took about a year off. I started training mixed martial arts in 1994 at the 'Minnesota Martial Arts Academy' and have been there ever since. We trained shoot wrestling, Muay Thai, kickboxing and wrestling. My influences were the early wrestlers like Dan Gable, and the early UFC wrestlers Dan Severn, Mark Coleman and Ken Shamrock.

Q: When did you first come across the UFC?

Sean Sherk: The first UFC I ever saw was UFC number 2. I think this was the first to be on pay-per-view, which was with Royce Gracie and Ken Shamrock in a 16-man tournament. That pretty much drove me to go and find a gym and train. I was real fortunate that one of the phenomenal gyms was here in Minnesota, which was only 20, 30 minutes from my house.

I trained with Greg Nelson back then and we would train shoot wrestling, he was also a wrestler and had a submission background in addition to having a Thai boxing background. So he had all three arts which I started training in, and training mixed martial arts. When I showed up at his academy I talked to him for five minutes and took a class. I knew I was in the right place as soon as I showed up, it just felt right. So Greg Nelson had a big influence on me, and we've got tons of great fighters at the academy coming through the ranks now.

Q: How did you get involved in the UFC?

Sean Sherk: I believe my first MMA fight was in 1999 when I fought in a smaller show. I also fought in local shows before making the transition into the UFC. I was just winning all of my fights. I think after my eleventh win I got a phone call from

Monte Cox, who at the time was a big figure in mixed martial arts world, and he still is. He asked me if I wanted to fight in the UFC. I said, "Alright, man! That's a dream come true for me!" So, like everybody else, I worked myself up and my first fight was at UFC 30 [against Tiki Ghosn], which I won. It was a one fight deal so they didn't use me any more for a while, so I went back fighting in the smaller shows until I was 19 when I ended up signing a three fight contract with the UFC.

Q: What was the difference between fighting in the unforgiving arena of the UFC compared to the wrestling tournaments you were accustomed to?

Sean Sherk: It's all a sport based theme, that's what I love to do and the love for competition and sports that I have is ingrained in me. The difference is that in wrestling if you get beat once or twice in a season, those losses go away and you start fresh again. But with something like mixed martial arts, when you get beat, it stays on your record for life. So I think the wins and the losses are a lot more important in the aspect and also because it's my job I do this for a living. I always had the goal to win the UFC title. Wins and losses make a difference.

Q: On April 25th 2003, you were given a title shot against the welterweight champ Matt Hughes. Was this a tough fight for you?

Sean Sherk: Yes, it was a huge fight! He was regarded by many as pound-for-pound the best fighter in the world at the time, and I was a huge underdog, 5-1 I think. Nobody really gave me a whole lot of a chance. As I've always said, I trained really hard for that fight and came out and fought, and although I ended up getting beat I earned a lot of respect from the fans and the fighters.

Q: Can you tell me about your experiences fighting in Japan?

Sean Sherk: Pride was probably the biggest show in the world, they were selling out the Tokyo Dome; a 20,000 arena was considered a small show. Pride was a pretty big deal and I got a two fight deal, but the money wasn't good so we just ended up taking the one fight. I fought one of their champions over there, [Ryuki] Ueyama. My goal was to go over there and show the Japanese fans and the promoters of Pride who I was, make a name for myself and become a mainstay with the show. Unfortunately, after I won the fight they chose not to sign me anymore.

Q: At one point in your career you actually packed it all in because you said you were not getting enough fights. Is it true you went out and found a normal job?
Sean Sherk: What happened was, I got let go from the UFC after I got beat by Matt Hughes, and I also stopped fighting in the small shows and went to Japan to fight in Pride where I beat one of their top guys - but they chose not to re-sign me! So I was stuck fighting in a lot of smaller organisations and could not get big fights. None of the top guys would fight me; I was a real dangerous fighter to fight in a smaller show, because the money wasn't right. So I couldn't get fights and opponents, so after my kid was born I basically said, "I can't do this anymore." So I walked away from the sport and got a normal job, flooring.

Q: Do you think as the sport evolves the athletes will be paid mega-bucks?
Sean Sherk: I hope so, I really do, and I hope it changes during my time because I would like to get those pay days I deserve too. Right now you've got a lot of big shows coming on the scene like Affliction, EliteXC and they're all trying to compete with each other - and, with competition, it drives up wages for the fighters because you've got people competing for us. I really hope the pay days get better because I don't want to go

back to work in a full time job after this.

Q: You finally got a fight for the lightweight belt at UFC 64 on December 2006. You beat Kenny Florian, what do you have to say about that win?
Sean Sherk: That was my first fight as a lightweight in the UFC. They basically gave me a title shot which was good. My credentials at the welterweight level have always been real good so they gave me the shot against Kenny Florian. He is a well rounded fighter with good jiu-jitsu and striking skills. We went out there and did our thing and I was able to pull the fight off and win the belt.

Q: What motivates you to fight and compete in the cage?
Sean Sherk: I've always been a super jock, I loved wrestling, playing football, baseball, lifting weights. I was into sports my entire life, so being a professional athlete was always a dream of mine. This is a dream come true for me. Being a professional athlete and being able to make a living doing something I love is a dream come true. I can't complain.

Q: You have a unique training regime which includes some fascinating drills such as the tyre flips, and gorilla drills, can you explain what exactly these are?
Sean Sherk: That's part of the caveman training that I do APL, with my conditioning coach. He comes up with different training regimes for me to do, conditioning drills etc. If you look at a fight, you use different muscles, so many different types of cardio, different type of exercises, I work with my conditioning coach a couple of times a week and he puts me through just a bunch of different programmes; no schedule is exactly the same, as this keeps your body guessing.

The Sledgehammer drill is going to work some cardio and power; a lot of boxers do this as well by chopping wood. It teaches you to use your entire body for power. The Gorilla drill

- that's another one where you use your body and just great for cardio. We like to end our training with this kind of stuff and we go real hard for 4-and-a-half minutes and spend 30 seconds doing gorilla drills.

Q: So far what has been the best part of your UFC career?
Sean Sherk: My best moment has to be winning the belt. For me it was a dream come true. Something I worked for a very long time and everything I'd been through in mixed martial arts, it was something I didn't think would happen at one point. At one point, I actually walked away from the sport, but winning the belt was definitely the defining moment of my career.

Q: Is it OK to talk me through your day-to-day activities?
Sean Sherk: When I'm training for a fight basically all I do is train. I get up in the morning eat my breakfast and hang out with my family a little bit, then I go to the gym usually around 11.30am. I work out two or three times a day depending on what the day's schedule is.

Each day I do different stuff, I train six days a week for about 12 weeks before a fight. When preparing for a fight, it is physically and mentally grueling, so when you are not training for a fight I like to get away from it and just relax and hang out with my kids, and try to do some fun stuff that I like to do. In winter time, I go snow mobiling; in the summer, I go paintballing on the weekends. I try to get some good activities and hang out with the family and eat normal food.

Q: Your fight with Hermes Franca at UFC 73 became controversial as both fighters were tested positive for performance enhancing substances. You have always denied taking any illegal substances. Can you comment on this issue?
Sean Sherk: Basically they accused me of taking nandrolone. I had 12 milligrammes in my system and the cut off limit is 6. I

didn't do it! So I went through the appeal process and I did everything to prove I hadn't taken anything. I had blood tests done which is a lot more accurate for steroids because it stays in the system longer and it's easier to find in the blood. I went to the lie detector test which I took three times and passed it all three times. My lawyer went through the whole entire testing process.

They made a lot of mistakes in the testing process. They found that there was actually carry over in the machine they were testing in, they tested everyone's sample in the same machine and they suppose to clean the machine out between tests. Three people were tested before me for steroids. When it was my turn the machine did not read zero, there were still steroids in the machine and they ran my sample anyway.

I just find it kind of funny after that entire process. After it was all over with, the California Commission let Quest laboratories, which was the lab which ran the samples. They then reduced my sentence from a year to 6 months which is pretty much saying they are not willing to overturn it. It was just a really bad situation to be in. I lost my belt to a lot of scrutiny and a lot of stuff from fans. It's all over with now and I'm ready to move on.

Q: Any comments on your loss to BJ Penn at UFC 84?
Sean Sherk: My goal was to try to exploit his cardio and making him tired. I thought I could out point him in the first couple of rounds on the feet, and then start shooting on him in the later rounds when he got tired. But his cardio was pretty good for that fight and the best I'd seen. He wasn't breathing really heavy, he was standing between rounds and not sitting down. So he trained for this fight and knew I was going to try to run him out of gas so he trained hard for it. He was a better fighter that night. I've always got along with BJ until we were preparing for this fight; it's just one of those things. I don't take things personally I know it's just a sport. I want that belt back I

can say that for sure. If he decides to stay in the 155lbs division then I want to fight him again.

Q: Any particular fighter you would like to fight in the UFC?
Sean Sherk: Right now, for me who ever makes sense I'll fight. I just fought BJ Penn who is one of the biggest names in the sport and I lost my belt and I want to get that belt back. I'll fight someone who is a contender who has been around for a while and someone who is a big name.

Q: How many years do you have left in fighting?
I really don't know how many more years I have left, it depends on my body but I feel pretty good physically. Maybe I would open up a gym in the future and train fighters who can be world champs one day.

Q: What's your relationship with Brock Lesnar?
Sean Sherk: I don't work out with him because he's too big for me to work out with. He's a physical specimen, a phenomenal athlete and he's got all the attributes of a middleweight and a heavyweight. He's going to be a force to be reckoned with. He learns really fast and he's picking this game up fast and he's got a very strong wrestling background along with his athletical ability he's going to be hard to deal with.

Q: Before the UFC came on the scene the general public had less respect for martial artists, how have things changed?
Sean Sherk: I think people understand the sport a lot more now, because everywhere you go you see it. You read about it and see it and people are learning and understanding what the sport is all about. People understand how hard we work and how well rounded we are as athletes - and people respect that. With the growth of the sport there's more understanding.

Remember that I've been fighting for nine years, before anybody knew what it was all about. Back in the early days, people didn't know even what mixed martial arts was, and I didn't tell people what I did because I didn't want to stand there for 20 minutes explaining. I didn't fight in Tough Man competitions because that's what most people thought it was, they had no idea what mixed martial arts was. People understand a lot more now because they see it a lot more.

Q: Anything you would like to add?
Sean Sherk: I would like to thank the Minnesota Martial Arts Academy and all the guys who train with me and help me get ready for a fight. I couldn't do any of this stuff if it wasn't for those guys. Also I would like to thank all my sponsors and my loyal fans.

FIGHTERS WEBSITES

Randy Couture	www.thenatural.tv
Matt Hughes	www.matt-hughes.com
BJ Penn	www.bjpenn.com
Chuck Liddell	www.icemanmma.com
Michael Bisping	www.bisping.tv
Ken Shamrock	www.kenshamrock.com
Royce Gracie	www.roycegracie.tv
Wanderlei Silva	www.wanderleisilva.com
Matt Serra	www.serrajitsu.com
Forrest Griffin	www.forrestgriffin.com
Frank Shamrock	www.frankshamrock.com
Jens Pulver	www.jenspulver.com
Keith Jardine	www.meanstyle.com
Tito Ortiz	www.titoortiz.com
Tim Sylvia	www.tim-sylvia.com
Sean Sherk	www.seansherk.com
Rashad Evans	www.jacksonsmma.com
Mark Coleman	www.teamhammerhouse.com
Dan Severn	www.dansevern.com
Georges St Pierre	www.gspfightclub.com
Antonio Nuguera	www.minotauro.net
Quinton Jackson	www.rampage.tv
Anderson Silva	www.spidersilva.com
Vitor Belfort	www2.uol.com.br/ vitorbelfort/2007/

Other websites

www.ufc.com
www.afflictionclothing.com
www.elitexc.com
www.cagerage.tv
www.sinisterbrand.com
www.whitecm.com
www.mmaagents.com
www.drivingforcesports.com
www.jacksonsmma.com
www.gracieacademy.com
www.rodrigogracie.com
www.spiritwingchun.com
www.ronbalicki.com

ABOUT THE AUTHOR

**FIAZ RAFIQ is a major columnist for Britain's
bestselling number one martial arts magazine 'Martial
Arts Illustrated' and contributor to 'Impact' - The
Global Action Movie Magazine.**

His work has appeared in magazines in the USA, UK, Australia,
Germany and France and also on the UFC section on the 'Sun'
website. He has worked on numerous Bruce Lee related projects
promoting the legendary iconic figure's legacy. He's also
appeared as a background artist in television shows and movies,
and qualified in Close Protection (Bodyguard).

Fiaz is the founder and director of HNL Media Group a company
dedicated to Publishing Sports related books. He is also the UK
PR agent for the legendary UFC fighter Royce Gracie.

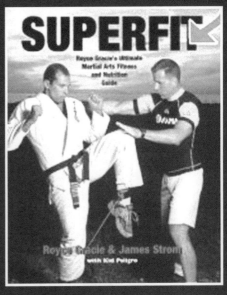

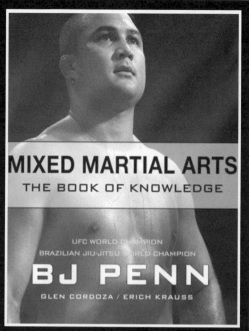
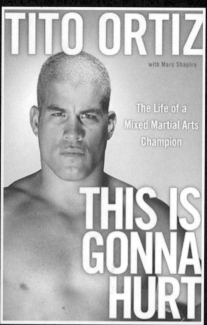

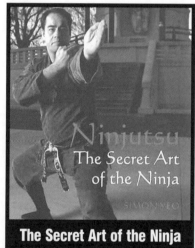